PROJECT MANAGEMENT
ESSENTIALS

FOURTH EDITION

PROJECT MANAGEMENT ESSENTIALS

A Quick and Easy Guide to
the Most Important Concepts
and Best Practices for
Managing Your Projects Right

WILLIAM P. ATHAYDE ◆ RUTH ELSWICK ◆ PAUL LOMBARD
DEBORAH BIGELOW CRAWFORD, EDITOR

MAVEN HOUSE

Published by Maven House Press, 4 Snead Ct., Palmyra, VA 22963; 610.883.7988; www.mavenhousepress.com.

Special discounts on bulk quantities of Maven House Press books are available to corporations, professional associations, and other organizations. For details contact the publisher.

Library of Congress Control Number: 2018945650

Paperback ISBN: 978-1-938548-97-0
ePUB ISBN: 978-1-938548-98-7
ePDF ISBN: 978-1-938548-99-4
Kindle ISBN: 978-1-947540-00-2

Printed in the United States of America.

CONTENTS

List of Exhibits   vii

Acknowledgements   xi

Foreword   xiii

Introducing . . . Project Management!   1

1   Selecting the Right Projects   13

2   Initiating the Project   25

3   Planning to Succeed   45

4   Project Cost and Budget   59

5   Scheduling the Project   83

6   The People Side of Project Management   103

7   Managing Project Risk   117

8   Executing the Project   143

9   Monitoring and Controlling the Project   161

10 Closing the Project   177

11 Lessons Learned . . . And Used   191

References   205

Suggested Readings   207

Index   213

About the Authors and Editor   223

LIST OF EXHIBITS

I-1   The Five Project Management Processes   2

I-2   Project Management Processes and Sub-Processes   3

I-3   Project Management Knowledge Areas   4

I-4   What Does a Project Manager Do?   8

I-5   Project Management is a Changing Profession   9

1-1   The Project Portfolio Management Process   14

1-2   Project and Portfolio Management Integration   17

1-3   PPM Capability Yields Benefits to the Organization   21

2-1   Elements of a Project Charter   27

2-2   Stakeholder Management Process   31

2-3   Influence/Impact Balancing Matrix   33

2-4   Stakeholders Engagement Assessment Matrix   37

2-5   Project Repository Documents   40

2-6   Kickoff Meeting Agendas   43

3-1   Project or Product? A Comparison of Deliverables   46

3-2   The Triple Constraint   49

3-3   Customer Priority Matrix   50

3-4   Work Breakdown Structure in Outline Format   52

3-5   Work Breakdown Structure Decomposed   55

3-6   Resource Assignment Matrix: Tyke Treat Meal   57

4-1   Types of Direct Costs   63

4-2   Cost Estimating Methods   67

4-3   Example of a PERT Estimate   69
4-4   Estimator's Checklist   73
4-5   The Cost Estimating Process   75

5-1   Simple Gantt Chart   87
5-2   ADM/PERT Chart   89
5-3   Schedule Management Process   91
5-4   PDM/CPM Chart   96
5-5   Lag Time   100
5-6   Lead Time   101

6-1   Differences Between Groups and Teams   106
6-2   Leadership Styles   109

7-1   Risk Management Process   122
7-2   Toyota's Five Whys Root Cause Analysis   124
7-3   Cause and Effect Diagram   125
7-4   Nine-Block Matrix   127
7-5   Pairwise Comparison Matrix   129
7-6   The Tornado Diagram   131
7-7   Decision Tree   132

8-1   List of Items to Review in a Documentation Review   146
8-2   Risk Log   151
8-3   Scope Change/Impact Request Form   152
8-4   Project Change Log   153
8-5   Project Change Log Instructions   154
8-6   Weekly Project Status Report   158

9-1   Potential Impact of the Butterfly Effect   163
9-2   The Plan-Do-Check-Act Cycle   165
9-3   Phase Review Process   166

9-4   Project Dashboard   168

9-5   Resource Bar Chart   169

9-6   Percentage over Budget Run Chart   169

9-7   Pareto Diagram of Defect Causes   170

9-8   Project Budget Bar Chart   171

9-9   Control Action Matrix   175

10-1 Project Closeout Checklist   183

11-1 Project Lessons Learned Questionnaire   195

11-2 Team Questionnaire for Capturing Lessons Learned   197

ACKNOWLEDGEMENTS

A "BOOK-BY-TEAM" is challenging under any circumstances, but when the team is geographically dispersed and has many other priorities, press day is that much more of a triumph. The editor and primary authors had much support, guidance, and help from others at PM Solutions, PM College, and Maven House Press – not to mention from their long-suffering families!

Thanks to Jeannette Cabanis-Brewin, editor-in-chief for PM Solutions Research, for serving as project manager and editorial "mother hen" to all the contributors. And special thanks to Jim Pennypacker and Maven House for the book design and elegant exhibits.

Above all, thanks to the many participants in courses who, over the years, have helped us to refine our methods of teaching project management essentials. Without you, this book would not exist.

William P. Athayde
Ruth Elswick
Paul Lombard
Deborah Bigelow Crawford

FOREWORD

I T'S OFTEN SAID that change is the one constant in life. Thus, here we are once again revising this book to embrace the changes that are evolving in the world of project management . . . and what an evolution it is!

Project management has been around for years – some might argue, for centuries. Most civil engineering programs had a course or two on the subject. But the genesis of project management, as we know it today, started back in 1969 at the 3 Threes Restaurant in Philadelphia. It was there that, after a series of discussions, a new organization for project managers to associate, share information, and discuss common problems was formed. The thought leaders who made this decision were the founders of the Project Management Institute, which is now one of the fastest-growing professional associations in the world. Through PMI and other related associations, the secret has been revealed: project management can improve the efficiency and effectiveness of organizations by putting a disciplined methodology behind the projects that are used to execute organizational strategies. Project management is a spoke in the wheel of strategy execution. It is not, however, the only spoke. Project, program, and portfolio management are all spokes in the wheel driven by organizational strategies, albeit differing in the way each contributes to the achievement of strategic goals. All three are critical to the success of most organizations and, unfortunately, some organizations don't know it.

The concepts of project management presented in this book are not rocket science. They are all common sense. Yet they require knowledge and discipline – a framework to do projects right, and the will to adhere to it. Those who internalize the precepts of project management and model them in their organizations have the potential to do great things . . . using these simple tools.

As you venture on this journey of learning, I hope that new doors and perspectives are opened for you. This book is purposely written in short, clear chapters, with the hope of making project management more easily understood. The authors, all valued senior instructors of PM College, use both their business experience and their academic backgrounds to make these chapters come alive. Your journey into the pages of this book isn't just a personal one, but rather one that we hope will be the start of you sharing what you've learned with others and adding value to whatever projects you participate in.

Deborah Bigelow Crawford
President, PM College
Glen Mills, Pennsylvania
July 2018

INTRODUCTION

Introducing . . .
Project Management!

PROJECTS ARE:

◆ Temporary endeavors undertaken to create unique products, services or results (PMI 2017, p. 4)

◆ Activities organized to deliver something of value to a customer (and therefore to your organization)

◆ The building blocks in the design and execution of your organization's strategies

As unique efforts, with deadlines, specific requirements or expectations, and budgets, projects differ from ordinary operations – the activities and actions that your organization does over and over again in the same way. These differences, and a framework for addressing them, form the basis for the project management standards published by the Project Management Institute as *A Guide to the Project Management Body of Knowledge,* or *PMBOK® Guide,* which you'll see referenced throughout this book. Briefly, project management consists of five Process Groups (see Exhibit I.1):

◆ Initiating Process Group

◆ Planning Process Group

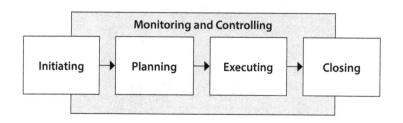

Exhibit I-1. The Five Project Management Processes

- ◆ Executing Process Group

- ◆ Monitoring and Controlling Process Group

- ◆ Closing Process Group

These five processes comprise forty-nine sub-processes (see Exhibit I.2), which interact with each other, may or may not be performed in a particular order, and are often iterative – some projects may go through several of the processes two, three, or more times before closing. These sub-processes are also organized into Knowledge Areas (see Exhibit I.3). We'll discuss these processes in more detail throughout this book.

The five Process Groups are carried out over the life cycle of a project, which goes through several phases (sometimes called stages). These phases may be defined differently for different industries, project types, and organizations. They begin with the concept development for the project and proceed sequentially through project closure. Examples of phases include the following:

- ◆ Assess–Define–Plan–Build–Test–Deploy–Manage–Close

- ◆ Concept–Design–Working Drawings–Bid–Construction

- ◆ Strategy–Preparation–Design–Development–Testing–Training–Support–Close

The phase structure allows the project to be divided into logical groups of activities, making it easier to plan, manage, and control the project. They're similar to the five Process Groups, but it's likely that most or all of the processes will be executed in some form in each phase.

PROJECT MANAGEMENT PROCESSES AND SUB-PROCESSES

Initiating	Planning	Executing	Monitoring and Controlling	Closing
Project charter	Project plan	Project work execution	Project work monitoring and controlling	Project closeout
Stakeholder identification	Scope plan	Project knowledge management	Integrated change control	
	Requirements collection	Quality assurance	Scope validation	
	Scope definition	Project team acquisition	Scope control	
	Work breakdown structure (WBS)	Project team development	Schedule control	
	Schedule plan	Project team management	Cost control	
	Activity definition	Communications management	Quality control	
	Activity sequence	Risk response	Resources control	
	Activity resource estimate	Procurement	Communications control	
	Activity duration estimate	Stakeholder engagement	Risk control	
	Schedule development		Procurement control	
	Cost plan		Stakeholder control	
	Cost estimate			
	Budget			
	Quality plan			
	Resources plan			
	Communications plan			
	Risk plan			
	Risk identification			
	Qualitative risk analysis			
	Quantitative risk analysis			
	Risk response plan			
	Procurement plan			
	Stakeholder plan			

Exhibit I-2. Project Management Processes and Sub-Processes

PROJECT MANAGEMENT KNOWLEDGE AREAS	
✓ Project Integration Management	✓ Project Resource Management
✓ Project Scope Management	✓ Project Communications Management
✓ Project Schedule Management	✓ Project Risk Management
✓ Project Cost Management	✓ Project Procurement Management
✓ Project Quality Management	✓ Project Stakeholder Management

Exhibit I-3. Project Management Knowledge Areas (PMI 2017)

A change to the sixth edition of the *PMBOK® Guide* was the acknowledgement that many organizations are embracing iterative and adaptive methods, including the agile methodology. These methods do not replace project management but add speed, flexibility, and creativity to the processes. While some organizations seek to implement a pure agile approach, most judiciously apply elements of it to make their project processes more adaptive to markets, risks, and resource issues. These hybrid approaches are an additional proof of the old concept that there's no one way to manage a project. Some organizations have policies that standardize the way projects are to be managed, while some allow the project team to choose the most appropriate approach. It all depends on the type of project, the sophistication of the project team, and the culture of the organization.

A History Lesson

Project management – thought of as a work effort with a specific set of requirements and a deadline – has been around since the days of the pyramids. However, the concept of the project as a management specialty – with its own techniques, tools, and vocabulary – had its beginnings in the 20th-century military. Like many other features of post-World War II America, the project and its supporting tools and techniques were a spin-off of the modern war effort. These military origins help to explain why the initial focus in projects was on planning and controlling.

The earliest non-military uses of project management – in capital construction, civil engineering, and research and development – imposed the idea of the project schedule, project objectives, and project team on an existing organizational structure that was very rigid. Without a departmental home or a functional silo of its own, a project was often the organizational stepchild – even though it may have been, in terms of dollars or prestige, the most important thing going on. Thus was born the concept of the matrix organization, where people with similar skills are pooled for work assignments rather than only working with others in their department.

There's been a tremendous resurgence in interest in the discipline of project management in the last decade. The reason: Information technology, information services, and new product development organizations have "discovered" project management. A traditional part of the toolkit for construction and large government projects, project management now sparks interest wherever compressing time-to-market cycles is an issue – in other words, throughout the modern marketplace. As industries work hard to compress product life cycles, reduce costs, and improve the quality of their deliverables, they are increasingly turning to project management.

Thus, the extensively practiced and researched disciplines of project control systems and schedule development have now come to find a home in less traditional areas such as high-tech industries, where organizations are under increasing pressure to utilize product development funds more efficiently. There's been a shift of focus toward the business side of delivering high-tech products and services: a focus on the *process* and the *business* of managing projects.

With this microscope turned on the business side of information technology projects comes the bad news: many of them are not managed well. In all fairness, project success rates in other industries may not be that great either, but they haven't been subjected to the intense scrutiny that technology projects have been, for the simple reason that high-tech has been a big economic engine for our economy. The average large IT project runs 45% over budget, 7% over time, and delivers 56% less value than expected. One in six IT projects has an average cost overrun of 200% and a schedule overrun of 70%. Nearly 45% of those surveyed admit they're unclear on the business objectives of their IT projects (Bonnie 2015).

As IT moves out of the back office and into more mission-critical business processes, such as customer relationship management and e-commerce, the line between IT and other types of projects is blurring.

Why is this so important? Because time is money. In PMI's 2015 *Pulse of the Profession*, it was reported that organizations lose $109 million for every $1 billion invested in projects and programs (PMI 2015).

However, we are starting to see improvement in the amount of money that organizations are wasting due to poor project performance. PMI's 2018 *Pulse of the Profession* reports that there has been a 27% decrease in the amount of money organizations have wasted due to poor project performance. As of this research, 9.9% of every dollar invested is wasted, down from 13.5% in 2013 (PMI 2018).

You Have the Power

For those of us who work in the field, it has long been evident that a good project manager can make the difference between success and failure. And over the past decade, this experiential wisdom has been underscored by research. For the past six years, PMI has conducted research to determine which factors have the most impact on project success. Not surprisingly, cultural and human factors rise to the top of the list (PMI 2018):

◆ A culture that supports the relationship between project managers and executive sponsors

◆ A roadmap of skills and actions for the executive sponsor

◆ Training to prepare executive sponsors to become actively engaged

◆ Avoiding scope creep by establishing a credible feedback loop with the customer

Similarly, in our *Project Manager Skills Benchmark 2015* study (PM Solutions Research 2015), we found that organizations with highly-skilled project managers display better project and business outcomes. Both executives and project managers agreed that leadership skills were by far the most important type of skill, rating them higher than basic project management skills, business skills, or industry expertise. Most striking, high-performing organizations rated listening and communicating the most important skills of all. And, while good project managers were deemed crucial to the organization, participants in the study agreed that the majority needed improvement in almost every skill (for most skills from 10%–20% improvement).

To sum up: we see positive returns on the investments that organizations are making in these project manager skill areas. This book is your start in the investing process.

What Does a Project Manager Do?

The project manager's role is a blend of "the art" of project management with "the science" of the discipline – a complex interweaving of technical, leadership, and strategic and business management skills.

- ◆ **Technical Project Management** (the science): It includes the knowledge, skills, and behaviors of project management and plans, work breakdown structures, Gantt charts, standards, critical path method/precedence diagrams, controls variance analysis, metrics, methods, earned value, s-curves, risk management, status reporting, and resource estimating and leveling. This is the technical aspect of the project manager's role.

- ◆ **Leadership** (a key component of the art): It includes that part of the project manager's role that involves guiding, motivating, and directing the team to help the organization achieve its business goals. These skills include effective communications, trust, values, integrity, honesty, sociability, leadership, staff development, flexibility, decision-making, perspective, customer relations, problem solving, managing change, managing expectations, training, mentoring, and coaching.

- ◆ **Strategic and Business Management** (a category that spans art and science): It includes skills that allow the project manager to see the organizational perspective and to negotiate and implement actions that align with the organization's strategic goals. In this role, the project manager should be knowledgeable enough about the essential business aspects of a project, able to develop an appropriate delivery strategy, and able then to implement in a way that maximizes the business value. Business management skills require an entrepreneurial awareness, financial skills, organizational savvy, and a big-picture focus.

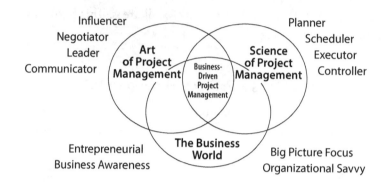

Exhibit I-4. What Does a Project Manager Do?

Exhibit I-4 shows how these areas interact. Another graphic explanation is provided by PMI's Talent Triangle, which demonstrates the need to have a balance of these three skill sets (see http://bit.ly/PMITalentTriangle).

Because of the nature of the enterprises that were early adopters of project management (military, utilities, construction industries), the profession grew up in an environment with a strong cost-accounting view and developed a focus on project planning and controls – an emphasis on the science. This is the kind of project management that we think of as being "traditional" or "classic" project management. However, the reality is that it probably represents an early evolutionary stage in the life of the discipline. More recently project management is being used in nearly all industries and across all functions within those industries.

Since then organizations have seen the emergence of countless trends. Organizations have flattened out, become matrixed, and new information technology has allowed people to communicate more effectively and reduce cycle times across all business processes. As a result, management began pushing more projects onto an increasingly complex organization, and the project manager suddenly became the jack-of-all-trades – forced to be everything to everyone. The role of project manager is now very demanding and requires an ever-expanding arsenal of skills, especially soft or interpersonal skills.

TRADITIONAL PROJECT MANAGEMENT	THE NEW PROJECT MANAGEMENT
Tactical	Strategically driven
Management of a single project	Integration, coordination, and control of multiple and prioritized projects
Project-wide and not necessarily cross-functional	Organization-wide and cross-functional
A discipline	An operating environment
A specialist function	A business philosophy integrated with project management

Exhibit I-5. Project Management is a Changing Profession

"New project management" is characterized by a more holistic view of the project, a view that goes beyond planning and controls to encompass business issues, procurement strategy, human resource issues, organizational strategic portfolios, and marketing. The new project management places its focus on leadership, communication, and strategic or business management capabilities rather than on a narrow set of technical tools. New project management advocates the use of the project management office to move corporate culture in a more project-oriented direction. (See Exhibit I-5)

You can't talk about the new project management without understanding how it has expanded and is linked to portfolio and program management. Portfolio, program, and project management are aligned with or driven by organizational strategies. Project management is used to develop and implement plans to achieve specific work that needs to be done, which is driven by the objectives of the program or portfolio that it's part of and, ultimately, to execute organizational strategies.

As a result, the role of the project manager has expanded in both directions: becoming both more business- and leadership-oriented on the one hand, while growing in technical complexity on the other. The widespread use of the project management office means that companies are now developing specialized project roles and career paths and defining specific competencies for these roles. Individuals who are gifted on the art side of the ledger – as program and project managers and mentors – can flourish, while those whose skill lies in the science of project management can specialize in roles that provide efficiency in planning and controlling projects.

According to research conducted by PM College in conjunction with Caliper International, 70% of the competencies of a project manager overlap with the competencies of a typical mid-level functional manager in Global 2000 organizations (PM Solutions Research 2002). This still holds true today. Most studies regarding competencies of a project manager conclude that you need a balance of technical, leadership and strategic/business management skills. These competencies include:

- **Leadership.** Whereas management focuses on systems and structures, short-range goals, and supervision of *when* and *how* work gets done, leadership focuses on people and relationships, takes a long-range view, and seeks to communicate why the work is worth doing. Leaders focus on developing people, creatively challenging the system, and inspiring others to act. Communication and negotiation are key leadership skills.

- **Problem-solving skills.** Project managers actively seek out information that might impact the project instead of waiting for it to surface, and they apply that information in creative ways. They must be able to both focus on the details of a problem and see it in the context of larger organizational or business issues.

- **Personal self-assessment.** Best practice project managers can consider their actions in a variety of situations and critically evaluate their performance. This introspective ability enables great project managers to adjust for mistakes, adapt for differences in team personalities, and remold their approaches to maximize team output.

- **Influencing ability.** Great project managers can influence others' decisions and opinions through reason and persuasion. They have the strategic and political awareness and the relationship development skills that are the basis for influence: the ability to get things done in an organizational context.

◆ **Efficiency.** The best project managers work efficiently to complete only what's necessary to deliver projects on time, within budget, and without sacrificing quality. They take the fewest possible steps to get things done. They follow the simplest possible methodologies, standards, procedures, and templates. Along with efficiency come good prioritization and organization skills.

◆ **Technological savvy.** Effective project managers are proficient in project management support tools – not only traditional project scheduling tools but email, calendar, and virtual meeting tools. And of course they must have a working familiarity with the technology important to the industry within which they work.

◆ **Project management knowledge.** Successful project managers know that communication, trust, and reliability are key elements to forming a winning project team. However, even with the right personal and professional attributes, the project manager must understand the concepts of project management well to be successful.

◆ **Personal attributes.** Effective project managers display certain personal traits that contribute to success as well. Some that have been identified in the literature include enthusiasm for the project and for project management, tolerance for ambiguity, the ability to manage change, a talent for building relationships with others, honesty, a desire to achieve, self-confidence, strong analytical skills, good judgment, and strategic thinking capabilities.

How to Use this Book

Project Management Essentials was developed as a textbook for the popular introductory course taught by PM College and is written by the instructors who regularly present the course. Obviously, if you're a student in this course, you'll follow your instructor's guidelines on the use of this textbook.

But if you're pursuing project management knowledge on your own, you may want to also invest in a copy of the *PMBOK® Guide, Sixth Edition,* in order to have additional background on each of the topics discussed. This standards document describes in detail how the various processes and Knowledge Areas interrelate; *Project Management Essentials* adds real-life details from the instructors' personal experiences that show how project management works in the real world. Alternating reading chapters of the *PMBOK® Guide* and related chapters in this book is an excellent way to gain basic knowledge of the project management discipline.

CHAPTER ONE

Selecting the Right Projects

BEFORE PROJECT SCHEDULING, budgeting, and tracking . . . before initiation and planning . . . before there is a project to manage . . . your organization must decide in which projects to invest. The most competent project manager in the world cannot generate all the value that rigorous project management can bring if the organization doesn't select the right projects. And although project selection may be outside the scope of responsibility of many project managers, it's important for even beginning project managers to understand how projects are selected and prioritized by the organization. In addition, project managers who hope to advance in their organizations or in their professions need to familiarize themselves with project portfolio management to add value to their role in the organization.

What is Project Portfolio Management?

Corporate strategy remains just a pipe-dream unless projects are initiated to move the company toward its strategic goals. Like players on a team, these projects must be coordinated with each other and with organizational realities and objectives. Project portfolio management (PPM) is the process that facilitates this coordination. Used effectively, PPM ensures

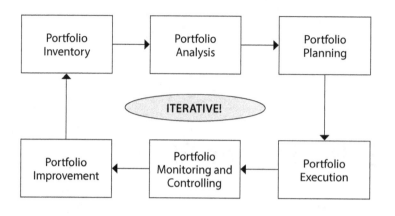

Exhibit 1-1. The Project Portfolio Management Process

that projects are aligned with corporate strategies and optimize the use of the organization's resources.

Unlike project management, which is focused on meeting individual project objectives, project portfolio management is concerned with managing a collection of projects, programs, and other work as a group to meet the organization's strategic objectives. PPM offers a holistic view of all the work that's planned and taking place in the organization.

Portfolio Management Processes

PPM comprises six key processes: portfolio inventory, portfolio analysis, portfolio planning, portfolio execution, portfolio monitoring and controlling, and portfolio improvement (see Exhibit 1-1). Organizations follow these processes to identify, categorize, monitor, evaluate, select, prioritize, balance, and authorize portfolio components within the portfolio (PMI 2013). PPM also includes processes for killing projects that no longer meet organizational objectives. The goal of portfolio management is to guide organizations on investment decisions; select projects to meet strategic objectives; facilitate decision-making transparency; prioritize resource allocation; realize the return on investment, and understand the risk profile of all projects and programs.

Portfolio Inventory

A portfolio is defined as projects, programs, subsidiary portfolios, and operations managed as a group to achieve strategic objectives. Portfolio management includes processes to evaluate, select, prioritize, and allocate resources with the hope of accomplishing the goals and strategies of the organization. (PMI 2017, p. 15)

An organization's portfolio inventory is simply a list of projects, programs, sub-portfolios, and other work that the organization has grouped together in order to see and manage the work as a whole. Initial project requests enter the portfolio inventory, where project data is captured and organized for portfolio analysis. That data might include a project ID, project name, project manager, project sponsor, start and end dates, estimated cost/budget, project priority, project benefits, level of effort needed to execute the project, project risk, and project status. (Note: PMI's portfolio management standard discusses these processes in slightly different terms, identifying three core processes that encompass the six discussed here. While the mapping/terminology is a bit different, the concepts align.)

Portfolio Analysis

In the portfolio analysis process, the organization aligns projects to business strategy, examining business and project risks, then selects which projects to work on and prioritizes them. The portfolio is reviewed periodically (monthly or quarterly) to analyze the projects for their fit, utility, and balance (and whether that's changed over time): Do the projects *fit* the organization's strategy? Do they have *utility* – value? And is the portfolio *balanced* – is the mix of projects optimized to deliver the greatest overall benefit to the organization? We'll discuss fit, utility, and balance in more detail later in this chapter.

Portfolio Planning

Once projects are selected and initiated, they enter the project planning phase. Here resources are allocated and projects are scheduled. Funding and resource allocation are based on the priority of the project. This project management process integrates with the portfolio planning process, where resource allocation and schedule decisions are made, taking into account the whole portfolio of projects.

Portfolio Execution

Portfolio execution is a process for implementing the portfolio of programs and projects by means of budgeted resource allocations and a focus on getting the work done efficiently and effectively. In order to execute quickly, in the correct sequence, the organization must pay close attention to its project capacity: Does the organization have enough resources, available at the right time, to effectively execute all the projects in its portfolio? An organization that's overloaded with projects becomes mired down as resources try to keep up by multitasking. The result is usually a devastating slowdown in project flow.

Portfolio Monitoring and Controlling

Organizations monitor project execution to ensure that out-of-control situations are quickly recognized and acted upon. Portfolio monitoring and controlling is a process for tracking the portfolio as projects are executed, detecting problems or changes in underlying premises, and reporting status to the appropriate management levels. In tracking the portfolio of projects, metrics are captured to assess the performance of each project. Reviews of the project portfolio involve a re-verification of the projects' critical success factors. In addition, shifting business, technology, and market conditions can re-arrange priorities. Re-planning may be required, including changes in resource allocation and scheduling. Project portfolio management is tightly integrated with project management.

Portfolio Improvement

Portfolio improvement is a process for making necessary adjustments to the portfolio, not once but iteratively and formally so that re-balancing and analyzing the portfolio become simply the way business is done. This process is dynamic, iterative, and ongoing and must be managed artfully

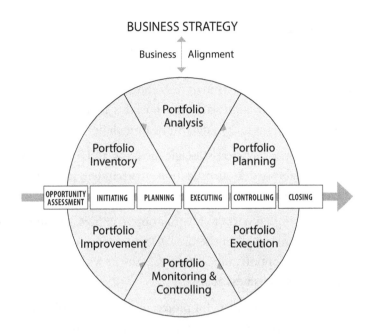

BUSINESS STRATEGY

Business | Alignment

Exhibit 1-2. Project and Portfolio Management Integration
Project portfolio management is tightly integrated with project management. These iterative processes occur throughout the project management life cycle through project and portfolio reviews.

depending on the project life cycles as well as organizational issues such as budget cycles.

As we've shown, project portfolio management is tightly integrated with project, program, and operations management. These iterative processes occur throughout the project life cycle through project and portfolio reviews. The role of the project management process within the organizational context of strategy and portfolio alignment is shown in Exhibit 1-2.

Project Selection: Fit, Utility, and Balance

Organizations focus on three elements in selecting and prioritizing the projects that they plan to execute: fit, utility, and balance (Bridges 1999).

17

Fit

The first major step in portfolio selection is to identify project opportunities and determine whether those opportunities are in line with the organization's strategies. This may consist of identifying and initially screening projects before more in-depth analysis is conducted. What is the purpose of the project? Does it align with your business strategy and goals? Actions that organizations take to determine fit include:

◆ Making sure that clear strategic direction and business goals have been established. In an execution environment, strategic focus becomes the foundation for selecting projects.

◆ Developing a process to identify opportunities, keeping it simple and easy to use all of the time. Organizations identify a team to review the opportunities and assess the fit with their strategic direction and business goals.

◆ Establishing a template for project justification. Project ideas need to have substance and content, otherwise it's difficult to screen the projects. The template includes things such as a description of the project, the sponsor, the link to strategy and business goals, and a high-level description of the project's costs, benefits, and risks.

◆ Establishing minimum acceptance criteria. There are basic requirements that projects must meet before they're considered for further analysis and funding. Such requirements may include the link to strategy, business threshold minimums (e.g., return-on-investment or cost/benefit ratio minimums), compliance with organizational constraints (e.g., existing technology architecture), and completion of the project justification template.

Utility

The second major step in portfolio selection is to further define the project (if needed) and analyze the details surrounding its utility. The utility of a project is typically defined by costs, benefits, and associated risks. Why should this project be pursued? What is the usefulness and value of the project? Actions that organizations take to determine utility include:

◆ Establishing common criteria to support decision making. Multiple projects vie for resources and funding, and somehow a decision has to be made on which ones to select.

◆ Making sure that accurate data is available to make decisions. In addition to establishing criteria, organizations must ensure that the data used to value each project is accurate and current.

◆ Measuring each project against the common criteria. Since most decisions are based upon multiple factors, organizations weight each criterion to establish its relative importance.

◆ Calculating a score for each project using its value for each criterion and applying the relative weights. The organization then ranks the utility of the project opportunities (along with ongoing projects in the portfolio) and uses this information to help them determine which projects to select and how to prioritize them.

Balance

The third step in portfolio selection is to consider the balance of projects in the portfolio. How does the project opportunity relate to the entire portfolio (in terms of cost, value, resource use, etc.) and how can the project mix be optimized? Actions that organizations take to determine balance include:

◆ Establishing a process that optimizes the portfolio, not just the individual projects. Industry approaches for developing portfolios range from simple ranking based on individual project financial returns to more complex methodologies that take into account the inter-relationships between projects.

◆ Considering all types of projects in building the portfolio – research, new product development, information technology, business improvement . . . and so on. Remember that relative comparisons are being made, not specific comparisons.

The key to successful project portfolio management is having an effective portfolio selection process, one that ensures that the organization's projects are aligned with corporate strategies, optimize the use of the organization's resources, and deliver maximum value.

19

Why Is PPM Important?

How work is done has changed faster than the way companies are managed, causing a disconnect between the ability to manage projects on the project level and the ability to manage them collectively on the enterprise level. There are powerful arguments for eliminating this disconnect.

No one would think of building a house by turning 100 different construction teams loose to build 100 different rooms, with no single blueprint or agreed-upon vision of the completed structure to go by. Yet this is precisely the situation in which many large companies find themselves when managing their projects. Companies routinely over-schedule their resources (human and otherwise), run redundant projects, and damage profitability by investing in off-topic activities that don't contribute to organizational value.

Applying effective PPM practices is becoming increasingly important to all business entities. Small or large, each organization must select and manage its investments wisely to reap the maximum benefits from its investment decisions. In the IT investment arena, IT executives are finding that senior management is demanding a tangible return from their large investment in information technology.

Organizations in many other industries are implementing project management practices to improve their ability to execute projects on time and within budget. Just as important as improving project management practices and organization, however, is the need to execute the right projects. Implementing an effective PPM process helps organizations select projects that support their business goals, diversify their investment, and maximize business performance. (see Exhibit 1-3).

The Project Portfolio Manager

The importance of PPM is underscored by the fact that PMI has established an additional practice standard for it, the *Standard for Portfolio Management, Third Edition*. For project managers who move beyond managing single projects, this standard helps to define the practice of PPM in much the same way that the *PMBOK® Guide* defines project

BENEFITS OF PROJECT PORTFOLIO MANAGEMENT					
Level of PPM Capability:	Level 1	Level 2	Level 3	Level 4	Level 5
✓ Project customers are satisfied	3.4	3.4	3.6	4.0	4.4
✓ Strategic plan better executed	3.2	3.5	3.8	4.3	4.6
✓ Resources allocated optimally	3.0	2.7	3.2	3.6	4.1
✓ Poor projects are killed	2.9	2.9	3.2	3.7	3.9
✓ Projects better aligned to strategy	3.6	3.8	4.2	4.4	4.3
✓ Working on the right projects	3.3	3.3	3.6	4.1	4.1
✓ Project redundancies eliminated	3.1	3.3	3.6	3.7	4.1
✓ Cost savings increased	3.1	3.3	3.6	4.0	4.1
✓ Risk is balanced across projects	2.7	2.7	3.0	3.8	4.3
✓ Profits increased	2.8	3.0	3.3	3.9	3.8
✓ Gaps in portfolio are managed	2.9	3.0	3.3	3.9	3.8

Exhibit 1-3. PPM Capability Yields Benefits to the Organization
Project management professionals were asked to rate the project portfolio
capability of their organization on a scale from one (immature) to five (best in class)
and indicate their level of agreement on the benefits of PPM to the organization, on
a scale from one (strongly disagree) to five (strongly agree). Clearly, organizations
with higher PPM capability see greater benefits.

management. Even if, at this point in your career, becoming a portfolio
manager is in the future, knowledge of the aspects of this role can play a
part in your personal development and aspirations. Recent editions of the
PMBOK® Guide acknowledge this increased pressure on project managers
to be strategic thinkers with an expanded focus on the business value of
projects. (PMI 2017).

Here's how PMI's portfolio management standard defines the role of
portfolio manager (PMI 2013):

The portfolio manager may be an individual, a group, or a governing
body and is responsible for establishing, monitoring, and managing
all assigned portfolios. Responsibilities include the following:

◆ Establishing and maintaining a framework and methodology

◆ Establishing and maintaining relevant portfolio management
processes

21

- Guiding the selection, prioritization, balancing, and termination of portfolio components to ensure alignment with strategic goals and organizational priorities

- Establishing and maintaining appropriate infrastructure and systems to support processes

- Continuously reviewing, reallocating, reprioritizing, and optimizing the portfolio

- Providing stakeholders with risk assessments

- Measuring and monitoring the value of the portfolio to the organization

- Meeting legal and regulatory requirements

- Participating in program and project reviews to reflect senior-level support, leadership, and involvement in key decisions

Practitioners who are interested in growing into the portfolio manager role should familiarize themselves with the publications cited in this chapter and in the suggested readings at the end of this book.

Project Portfolio Management Tools

There are many software applications for project portfolio management. Each year software developers improve the functionality of the tools to help portfolio managers organize their projects and programs, formulate their portfolio options, and analyze alternative scenarios. Pivot tables, bubble charts, resource allocation algorithms, and risk/reward diagrams offer portfolio managers a plethora of options and analytical capabilities.

Analytic software is still used successfully for prioritizing projects based on appropriate strategic criteria. Additionally, a number of software vendors provide tools that help in financial analysis and return-on-investment calculations. Today's tools are becoming extremely valuable in tracking and analyzing a portfolio, especially since disciplined project management provides a basis for collecting the information and data needed to plan and track the portfolio. However, it's important to remember that

PPM is a process that's set in motion by ideas (strategies) and based on decision making (What is most important now? In the future?), and it can't be done by simply implementing a tool. Indeed, even organizations with high capability and a high return on their PPM process investment are likely to use simple spreadsheets to carry out the nuts and bolts of tracking aspects of PPM (PM Solutions Research 2013).

WHILE EFFICIENT PROJECT EXECUTION is an essential factor in a business's success, in today's competitive environment successful project execution by itself is not enough. Organizational strategies and priorities are linked and have relationships between portfolios and programs and between programs and individual projects. Organizational planning impacts project prioritization based on risk, funding, and the organization's strategic plan. Sustainable competitive advantage won't come from only working efficiently on projects. Project portfolio management provides a consistent way to select the right projects, to ensure that projects and programs are reviewed to prioritize resource allocation, and to make sure that the portfolio is aligned to the organizational strategies.

CHAPTER TWO

Initiating the Project

What is Project Initiation?

NITIATION SIMPLY MEANS starting from the beginning with the tools that you need. Imagine a contractor arriving at a customer's lot to start building a custom home – with no blueprints, no signed contract, no site survey, and no knowledge of whether the client wants a one- or two-story house. Ludicrous? Obviously. Yet many projects are started with no charter, no clear goal, no boundaries defined, no idea of who the stakeholders are, and few solid client requirements. Initiation simply means having all the information you need to start the project off in the right direction.

The Project Charter

Creating a project charter is the first step in the right approach to managing a project. It formally announces that a project or phase has begun. It also serves to document the initial requirements that, if met, will satisfy the stakeholders' needs and expectations. The project charter, issued by a project sponsor, project management office, or portfolio steering committee, gives the project manager authority to apply resources to project activities. In the absence of a formal project selection process, the project manager may develop the project charter and give it to the sponsor for signature and transmission. Without this authority, the project manager may have difficulty in obtaining human resources or even funding. The important point to understand about chartering is that *it links the project to the ongoing work of the organization.* (See Exhibit 2-1 for a list of project charter elements with definitions and instructions on what information is needed to create the charter.)

There's no set format for a charter; it may be a formal document, a contract, or even an email. Inputs to the charter (information needed to help you create the charter) may include such items as:

◆ The business case for undertaking the project, including a description of expected outcomes.

◆ The benefits management plan that defines the processes to create and sustain the project benefits.

◆ Current enterprise environmental factors, such as the structure and culture of the organization, market conditions, and existing resources.

◆ Existing organizational process assets, such as formal and informal plans, processes, policies, and procedures currently used by the organization.

◆ Agreements to define initial project intentions. Agreements may be in the form of contracts, memorandums of understanding (MOUs), and other documents. Agreements may be written or verbal.

The information gathered from these items, aided by expert judgment in assessing the inputs, will help the project manager begin documenting the business objectives and customer needs that the project is intended to satisfy and how the product, service, or result delivered will satisfy those needs. This project charter will also list the stakeholders involved in the project, outline constraints that might limit the project team's options, and provide a detailed description of the scope of the project.

SUGGESTED ELEMENTS OF A PROJECT CHARTER (NOT INCLUSIVE)	
Elements	Definitions and Instructions
Project name	Enter a brief name to describe the project.
Project sponsor	This generally is the executive of the business area for which the project is being undertaken. This person is responsible for budgeting the funds to undertake the project and has final authority to approve project completion.
Project manager – responsibility and authority level	This is the person responsible for planning and managing the project.
Key stakeholder list	Identify the major stakeholders who will have the biggest impact, interest, etc. on the project.
Business background	Give an overview of the business reasons for the project.
Project purpose	Using business terminology, give a general description of the project scope (provide details in the following sections). Indicate both what is within the anticipated scope and what is outside the scope. Consider these topics: • Systems • Infrastructure • Communications • Business locations
Project exit criteria	The conditions to be met in order to close, or cancel, the project or phase.
Project approval requirements	Description of project success, who makes the decision on project success, and who signs off.
High-level requirements (deliverables)	List the specific, expected project deliverables and how these will meet the objectives. The deliverables should be as tangible as possible.
Summary milestone schedule	Major time frames.
Overall project risk	Uncertainty on the project as a whole.

Exhibit 2-1. Elements of a Project Charter

Project Management Methodology: Processes and Phases

Once the organization selects a project and the charter is issued, the project manager's primary job begins. Most project managers realize that there's more than one way to manage a project. The project management processes are a logical grouping of tools, techniques, and approaches with well-defined interfaces. However, in practice these groups overlap and interact in many ways that that will vary from project to project. The application of these processes is iterative throughout the life of the project, as well as through each phase. The project manager, together with the team, is responsible for determining how the processes will be applied:

- The initiating process defines and authorizes the new project or new project phase.

- The planning process defines and refines objectives and plans the course of action required to attain the objectives and scope that the project was undertaken to address.

- The executing process integrates people and other resources to carry out the project management plan for the project.

- The monitoring and controlling process regularly measures and monitors progress to identify variances from the project management plan so that corrective action can be taken when necessary to meet project objectives.

- The closing process formalizes acceptance of the product, service, or result and brings the project or a project phase to an orderly end.

Think about which of these processes are applied in your organization. In practice, if any of the process steps are not applied, it's a warning flag that the project may be entering troubled waters. Often students of project management ask, "I work on such small projects – do I really have to go through all these steps?" The response is a resounding "Yes!" The difference in the process steps between a large and small project is not whether the steps need to be followed, but how much time is spent on each step. For example, if you're painting a room in your house, you can jot down your entire plan on the back of an envelope. But it's still important to identify the deliverables – the amount of paint you'll need based on square footage, masking tape, brushes, rollers, etc. You estimate cost, resources, time, etc. – it just doesn't take as long to plan for a small project as it would for a large one. The size and type of project determine how much time you'll need to spend and how much detail you'll need to provide for each process step.

Very different from the Process Groups are project phases, but the two terms are often, erroneously, used interchangeably. Project phases are time bound, with a clearly defined start and finish, and they end in a deliverable. For example, if a project has a Requirements Definition Phase, the deliverable would be the requirements document. If there is an Execution Phase, the deliverable would be the product. There are no recommended phases, and what they are may be particular to the project or the organization.

Project Information

As if the project manager doesn't have enough to do, it's also important that he or she keep in mind that project information and data must be continually collected, analyzed, and distributed. Before a communication plan can be put in place it's important to understand the difference between data and information. Not understanding this difference is often the basis of the miscommunication that so often plagues project managers. The guidelines are as follows:

◆ Work performance data include raw observations and measurements that are collected during the project. For example, the change management system tracks the number of change requests, and an earned value system can track the percentage of work that has been completed.

◆ Work performance information is raw data showing exactly where you are in the project's status. Many project managers refer to it as the *as-of-now* status. It's how much time has elapsed, how much money has been spent, or how many resource hours you've used compared to what you had planned.

◆ Work performance reports are simply the way you distribute the project information. Examples of work performance reports include status reports, presentations, and emails.

One way to think about it is to say that work performance data involves gathering the information, work performance information analyzes that data and puts it into some kind of context, usually planned versus actual, and work performance reports present it to stakeholders in a way that they can understand it.

Engaging the Stakeholder

"What are some of your biggest project management challenges on the job?" When this question is posed to students of project management, inevitably one response will be "managing stakeholders." Whenever I hear this, I follow up with another question – "How do you define a successful project?" After a few puzzled looks at the apparent quick change of subject, students will reply with the standard "bringing in the project on time, within budget, meeting all the requirements" answer. Finally someone will respond with, "The project is successful when the customer is satisfied." *That's the answer I'm looking for.*

Isn't it amazing that many times, particularly on larger projects, team members don't know who their customer is? How can the customer be satisfied if team members don't know who they're trying to satisfy? At a bare minimum, team members, as well as the project manager, need to know who the client and sponsor are. The roles and responsibilities of these two key stakeholders will be discussed at greater length a little later in this chapter.

How does PMI's standards document define a stakeholder? According to the *PMBOK® Guide,* a stakeholder is an "individual, group, or organization that may affect, be affected by, or perceive itself to be affected by a decision, activity, or outcome of a project." That can cover a pretty wide range of people. Senior managers, vendors, contractors and subcontractors, partners, creditors, colleagues, and the general public are just a few of the many stakeholders frequently identified. The project manager

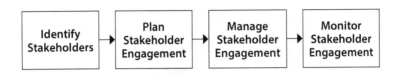

Exhibit 2-2. Stakeholder Management Process

acts as a traffic cop in the middle of the communication intersection, trying to make sure that information is flowing smoothly in all lanes of communication traffic. As children, many of us played a party game called telephone. One child would whisper a phrase into the ear of the next child, who in turn would whisper the phrase to the next child, and so on until the last child in line would stand up and reveal her understanding of the phrase. It was hilarious when the phrase didn't bear even the slightest resemblance to the original – but it isn't so funny in the project management environment when communication between stakeholders gets confused.

Exhibit 2-2 shows you the steps that you need to go through to engage your stakeholders.

Identifying Stakeholders

Identifying and engaging stakeholders can be one of the most difficult tasks the project manager has to perform. The first step in the process is to figure out who all the stakeholders are, which can be a challenge in itself. To take the first step you need to conduct a *stakeholder analysis.* Stakeholder analysis is a systematic gathering of information to determine whose interests should be taken into account throughout the project. A stakeholder analysis generally follows three steps:

1. **Identify your stakeholders by brainstorming or other data-gathering techniques.** Think of all the people who are affected by your work, have influence or power over it, or have an interest in its successful or unsuccessful conclusion. The brainstorming can be done with the project team, customer, sponsors, or others.

2. **Prioritize and categorize your stakeholders using the influence/impact balancing matrix** (see Exhibit 2-3). You may now have a long list of people and organizations that are affected by your work. Some of these may have the power to either block or advance the project's progress. Some may be interested in what you are doing, others may not care. The most important aspect of the stakeholder analysis is that it must be objective and fact-based, not based on preconceived judgments or assumptions. The expectations of customers, sponsors, and other key stakeholders need to be determined early in the project. Many project managers make the serious mistake of assuming that they know and understand the stakeholders' expectations when in fact they don't. Moreover, as the project progresses stakeholder expectations may change.

3. **Perform a stakeholder assessment.** This will allow you to strategize on how to influence your stakeholders in order to enhance their support and mitigate potential negative impacts.

The detailed information that you gather on the stakeholders should become part of a stakeholder register. This document might include information such as:

◆ **Identification information:** What position do the stakeholders hold in the organization? Where are they physically located? How can we contact them if we need to? What stakeholder role do they play?

◆ **Assessment information:** What are stakeholders' expectations for being engaged in the project? What are their communication needs?

◆ **Stakeholder classification:** Are they an internal or external stakeholder? How supportive are they of the project (leading, supportive, resistant, unaware, etc.)?

It's important to keep in mind that the stakeholders and their roles may change throughout the project; therefore the stakeholder register should be reviewed and updated routinely.

There are several types of stakeholders who need to be identified:

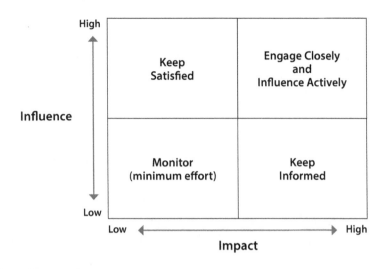

Exhibit 2-3. Influence/Impact Balancing Matrix

Key stakeholders

Key stakeholders (found on the upper right corner of the influence/impact balancing matrix) include the project manager, the customer/user, the team members, and the sponsor. They could also include members of the project management office, functional managers, and other influencers who are not directly related to the project but who, because of their position in the organization, may have an influence on the project. For example, on a manufacturing project the vice-president of marketing may have a voice in how the project should be approached and the priority it would have in the organization. The two most important key stakeholders, however, are the sponsor and the customer (Verzuh 2005):

* **Sponsors.** The sponsor's role is to help make the project, the project manager, and the project team successful. As a senior executive with formal authority who holds financial responsibility for the project, but who is independent of it, the sponsor uses his or her position and authority within the organization to act as a liaison between the project and the organization's decision-making

process. The sponsor uses formal authority and power on behalf of the project to provide advice or influence project priority. The sponsor's responsibilities may include issuing the project charter, reviewing the preliminary and final scope plans, reviewing and approving the project plan, ensuring that the right resources are available for the project, reviewing the priority of the project in relation to other projects within the organization, and generally helping the project manager to overcome organizational obstacles.

◆ **Customers.** The customer should get the first and last word on product description, budgeting, and acceptance criteria, since the customer pays the bills. Surprisingly, identifying the customer can often be difficult. In that case the project manager may need to look at some guidelines for dealing with various customer groups. First, the project manager must distinguish between the people with final authority over product requirements, those who must be consulted as the requirements are developed, and those who simply need to be informed what the requirements are. In industries whose products have many customers (software, pharmaceuticals, retail, etc.), the project manager must ascertain which departments should be included as stakeholders; for example, the project manager may choose the marketing department to represent the customer. Often in the public sector, such as in the Department of Transportation where the customers are all the people who use the highways, obviously not everyone can be listed as a customer. The best that can be done is to publish requirements, elicit public comments, follow the rules, and hope it all works!

Internal Stakeholders

Because these stakeholders are usually internal to the project organization, they are generally considered to be supportive of the project as well as the team. In practice, however, if the project manager doesn't have authority over team members or the project itself, this may not be a correct assumption. Examples of internal stakeholders include functional managers, project team members, and sponsors.

External stakeholders

Because these stakeholders are usually external to the project organization, they may not be supportive since they're not subject to the authority of the project manager. Again, in practice this may or may not be true. Project managers often find external stakeholders such as contractors and vendors to be much more supportive than internal resources.

Allies

Allies are stakeholders who are supportive of the project manager and the project team. No matter what goes wrong, allies will offer encouragement and any support that's required. They are stabilizers on the project and can be invaluable resources for the project team.

Opponents

Opponents offer roadblocks to the project manager as well as to the project team. It's never easy managing opponents, but with some foresight and planning it can be done. For example, several years ago I was offered the position of project manager on a project that had been around for ages. As a matter of fact, it was the laughingstock of the company, and people were always trying to get off the project. No one could even remember what the project goal was. Senior managers persuaded me to take on the project, convincing me that I could bring it to closure. Although I was given much-needed authority, these managers made it clear to me that the project team wouldn't change. They did agree, however, that since I didn't have the necessary technical expertise, a technical project lead would be added to the team so that I could focus on the project management side. I was delighted until I learned that my project lead was the former project manager. Clearly he had no interest in my success, and, even worse, the team was divided. Some of the team members were loyal to the former project manager, while others wanted me to succeed.

During our first team meeting the former project manager argued every point, no matter what I said. I felt drained after that meeting and knew that I had to get control of the situation quickly. I jotted down everything that the project manager had said and done in the meeting and saw something positive coming from my notes – there was a pattern to his behavior! Patterns are predictable, and therefore I could put together a plan to counter his sniping ways. The next meeting was important because three major decisions had to be made during the meeting. I put my plan into action by announcing to the team that these decisions had to be made in the meeting. I then broke them into two groups, with the former project manager leading the cons and another team member leading the pros. Then I reversed the process and had the former project manager leading the pros. By surprising him (he didn't anticipate that I would divide the team into two groups) I broke his pattern of behavior and didn't allow him to control the conversation. And as the leader of the pros group, he couldn't be negative.

Ambivalents

Ambivalent stakeholders sit on the fence. When things are going well, they're allies. When things are going poorly, they're opponents. The trick is to use them to your advantage when they're allies and plan for their behavior when you think they'll be opponents.

It's important that the project manager realize that all stakeholders are tuned in to one radio station – WIIFM (what's in it for me). The project manager, with the assistance of the team, ensures that the requirements and expectations of the stakeholders are identified and managed. Through the use of stakeholder management tools and discussions with the stakeholders, the project team will be better able to understand and manage those expectations.

The project manager should also identify stakeholder goals, particularly those of the key stakeholders. The project manager should do this analysis without the aid of the project team, although a trusted team member may offer helpful information. (In most situations a project manager would not want team members to know that a stakeholder was an opponent of the project or even ambivalent.) Analysis of stakeholder goals will help reveal the stakeholders as allies, opponents, or ambivalents.

STAKEHOLDERS ENGAGEMENT ASSESSMENT MATRIX					
Stakeholder	Unaware	Resistent	Neutral	Supportive	Leading
Sponsor				C	D
Project manager				D	C D
Team member 1				C D	
Team member 2				C D	
PMO director			C	D	
VP marketing	C			D	
VP finance		C	D		

Exhibit 2-4. Stakeholders Engagement Assessment Matrix
The letter C represents how well the stakeholder is currently engaged and the letter D represents the desired level of stakeholder engagement.

Planning Stakeholder Engagement

The next step in the stakeholder management process is to put a plan in place. In order to effectively plan communication and interaction, the current engagement level of all stakeholders should to be compared to the engagement level that's needed. The engagement level of stakeholders varies from being unaware of the project and potential impacts, to stakeholders who are both aware of the project and potential impacts and actively engaged in ensuring that the project is a success. In between these extremes, as in any bell curve, the majority of stakeholders may be:

◆ Resistant – aware of the project and potential impacts and resistant to change

◆ Neutral – aware of the project yet neither supportive nor resistant

◆ Supportive – aware of the project and potential impacts and amenable to change (PMI 2013)

Very often an assumption is made that each of the key stakeholders knows exactly what his or her role is. That's often an incorrect assumption. The current level of engagement of the stakeholders is documented using a stakeholders engagement assessment matrix (see Exhibit 2-4). The project team should contribute to determine the desired engagement level.

The result of stakeholder planning is the stakeholder management plan, which identifies the management strategies required to effectively engage stakeholders. It can be formal or informal, detailed or high level, based on the needs of the project. The stakeholder engagement plan may include the following:

◆ The desired and current engagement levels of key stakeholders

◆ The scope and impact of change to stakeholders

◆ Identified interrelationships and potential overlap between stake-holders

◆ Stakeholder communication requirements

◆ Reason for distribution of information

◆ A communication plan that defines when, how frequently, and how communication will take place for stakeholders

Manage the Stakeholder Engagement

As the project begins to move forward, the project manager will have to manage the stakeholders by communicating and working with them to meet their expectations, address issues, and get them engaged with the right activities at the right time. The key benefit of effectively managing the stakeholder engagement is that the project manager can increase support and minimize resistance from stakeholders to increase the chance of a successful project.

Successful stakeholder management and engagement require good monitoring of the relationship. That monitoring is known as controlling the stakeholder engagement. The key benefit of being able to control the stakeholder engagement is that it can increase the efficiency and effectiveness of the engagement activities as the project evolves and its environment changes. That control requires continually adjusting strategies and plans for engaging the stakeholders.

Project Repository

This document is primarily intended to help project managers focus on collecting the right kinds of data to make the most well-informed decisions for the project. The project repository has several aliases. It may be called the project workbook, the project file, the intellectual database, or something else. More important than the name, though, is that the document serves its purpose – a single source of information used to house all key information about the project. Either electronic or paper-based, the project repository:

- Serves as a central repository – data and information are not scattered throughout the organization, maintained by different people in different places
- Contains all the plans – all the information pertaining to the project
- Helps track changes to baseline plans – because all information is located here, it provides a way to monitor project progress and changes
- Serves as a communication source because it's easy to see changes and progress
- Aids in internal project audits and reviews

The project repository is a living document that should rely on a document control system so that changes can be tracked and the latest version used. Typically one person, who may or may not be a team member, should be in charge of the project repository, and access to the repository should be tracked. It should have each plan in a separate section for quick and easy access. The plans themselves should guide the project manager in collecting the right data. For each plan there should be a complementary section to store status reports.

Exhibit 2-5 shows a representative list of the contents of a project repository.

Don't build a bigger project repository than you need. The point is not to create a paper-consuming machine but to effect an efficient project management process (Ambler 2017).

Kickoff Meetings

Two of the most important project meetings you'll participate in are the kickoff meetings. These meetings are held soon after the contract is

DOCUMENTS FOUND IN A PROJECT REPOSITORY	
✓ Scope statement	✓ Resource plan
✓ Statement of Work (SOW)	✓ Communication plan
✓ WBS	✓ Risk management plan
✓ WBS Dictionary	✓ Roles and responsibilities
✓ Schedule	✓ Requirements documents
✓ Assumptions list	✓ Budget
✓ Organization chart	✓ Quality plan
✓ Change control plan	✓ Design documents
✓ Procurement plan	✓ Standards and procedures
✓ Status reports	✓ Lessons learned
✓ Meeting information	✓ Action logs
✓ Risk logs	✓ Issue logs
✓ Change requests	✓ Closeout reports

Exhibit 2-5. Project Repository Documents

awarded or a decision is made to initiate the project. There should be at least two types of kickoff meetings: the organizational kickoff meeting and the team kickoff meeting. Both are designed to get the project moving in the right direction and to begin establishing rapport among the team members and other stakeholders. These meetings don't have to be formal. Although the ideal situation is to have attendees in one place, the meetings may be held via conference calls or other virtual methods.

Organizational Kickoff Meeting

The organizational kickoff meeting should be attended by all key stakeholders, because this is when the initial review of the project scope and activities will take place. Its purpose is to allow all key stakeholders to become acquainted with the project as well as with each other. At a minimum the activities of an organizational kickoff meeting are as follows:

◆ Distribute the project charter. Remember that the project charter has been issued by the project sponsor, and it's at the kickoff meeting where the charter should be reviewed by team members and other key stakeholders.

- Introduce the team members. This is particularly important if team members and other stakeholders don't know each other or are involved in virtual teams. This should be done in an informal, fun way.

- Distribute a team/stakeholder roster. Include contact information for all team members and key stakeholders.

Team Kickoff Meeting

The team kickoff meeting allows all the team members to get acquainted. It should include the following activities:

- Introduce all team members. Again, this should be done in an informal, fun way. In this day of virtual teams, the meeting could be held via conference call.

- Establish roles and responsibilities. It's important to understand the difference between the two. *Role* defines who does what; *responsibility* defines who decides what. Team members need to understand what parts they will play as members of the team.

- Begin establishing the team charter. The team charter has nothing to do with the purpose of the project but determines how the team will operate – the rules of membership. It's vital in order to help minimize conflict and support record keeping and decision making within the team environment.

- Establish the team organizational chart. This provides a graphical representation of reporting relationships within the team.

- Begin establishing the project repository. This can begin with a review of the project charter and its inclusion as the first document in the repository.

Sample meeting agendas are shown in Exhibit 2-6.

Team Charter

Can you relate to this scenario? The team meeting has just begun, and two team members begin to argue a point. The argument goes on and on with no end in sight. Team members are bored and restless, and the project manager can't seem to get control. But if a time limit for discussions had been included in the team charter, then after the prescribed time of, say, three to five minutes, the discussion would have been halted and postponed to a later date.

One of the key project documents, often overlooked, is the team charter. The concept of a team charter should be introduced during the team kickoff meeting, and development should begin in that meeting or shortly after it. The team develops the charter to establish guidelines for how they will operate as a team. At a bare minimum the charter should consist of the following:

- **Administrative guidelines:** These have to do with how the project manager and the team handle day-to-day issues such as timekeeping, data collection, data management, communication, and anything else involving the administration of the project.

- **Ground rules:** These address the basic environment of the team. What are the expectations for interacting with other team members? Possibilities include: all team members will attend meetings or send a representative; no interrupting while another team member is talking.

- **Decision guidelines:** These keep the team from getting stuck. They should include time limits on discussions and when decisions will be made by the project manager or by the team.

- **Meeting guidelines:** These address how the team will conduct meetings. The guidelines will include things such as meeting times and locations, when agendas will be distributed, and who will keep meeting minutes.

Team charters are usually developed during the forming stage of team development and are primarily used during the storming stage. See chapter 6 for information on the five stages of team development.

SAMPLE ORGANIZATIONAL KICKOFF MEETING AGENDA

- Welcome — project manager (5 min.)
- Introductions — project manager (10 min.)
  - Project manager
  - Key stakeholders
  - Core team members
- Distribution of project charter — project manager (20 min.)
  - Review of project background and purpose including executive perspective
  - Review of project objectives/deliverables
  - Review of scope and schedule
  - Review of constraints and assumptions
- Roles & responsibilities — project manager (10 min.)
- Distribution of team/stakeholder roster (includes contact information) — project manager (10 min.)
- Questions/summary/closing — project manager (10 min.)

SAMPLE TEAM KICKOFF MEETING AGENDA

- Welcome — project manager (5 min.)
- Introductions/ice breaker — project manager (20 min.)
  - Project manager
  - Sponsor
  - Core team members
- Sponsor statement — sponsor (10 min.)
- Distribution of project charter — project manager (20 min.)
  - Review of project background and purpose
  - Review of project objectives/deliverables
  - Review of scope and schedule
  - Review of constraints and assumptions
- Assignment of team roles and responsibilities/team organization chart — project manager (15 min.)
- Description of team charter/ground rules — project manager (15 min.)
- Description of project repository content — project manager (10 min.)
- Distribution of team/stakeholder roster (includes contact information) — project manager (10 min.)
- Questions/next steps/closing — project manager (10 min.)

Exhibit 2-6. Kickoff Meeting Agendas (times may vary)

Now THAT THE project initiation groundwork is in place, let's move on to the nitty-gritty of project management: planning.

CHAPTER THREE

Planning to Succeed

A S THE SAYING GOES, "Customers don't always know what they want, but they know what they don't want when they see it." This saying is appropriate to project planning since one obstacle that project managers face is the difficulty of gathering requirements and doing the planning up front. Customers often smile indulgently at the team and say, "That planning stuff is okay, but let's just get started on the project." The consequences of this approach are increased time, more money, decreased quality, lower team morale, and numerous other difficulties. To fail to plan is to plan to fail, so project managers must work with customers to get them on board for all the steps of sound planning.

Although most project managers will declare loudly that one of the keys to project success is to make sure that the scope is clearly defined, most of them will barely whisper that how it's done is important as well. Enter the scope management plan, which is a part of the project management plan. The key word to keep in mind when thinking of the scope management plan is "process." Components of the scope management plan include processes for preparing a detailed scope statement, developing and maintaining the work breakdown structure (WBS), obtaining approval for deliverables, and determining how change requests relating to

PROJECT SCOPE	PRODUCT SCOPE
Measured against the plan	Measured against specifications
✓ Scope definition	✓ Drawings
✓ Schedule	✓ Software programs
✓ Budget	✓ Requirements
✓ Resource allocation	✓ Product description
✓ Risk management	✓ How it will be used
✓ Issues management	✓ Cost to own and operate

Exhibit 3.1. Project or Product? A Comparison of Deliverables
Product scope refers to the features and functions of the final output. Project scope refers to the work that needs to be done to accomplish the final output.

scope will be linked to the change control process. It's appropriate here to mention that PMI has traditionally emphasized what is called the *predictive* approach. In the latest *PMBOK® Guide* there is recognition that the *adaptive/agile* approach is realistic for many projects.

Defining Scope

The *PMBOK® Guide* glossary clearly differentiates between project scope and product scope. Project scope is defined as "the work performed to deliver a product, service, or result with the specified features and functions." Product scope is defined as "the features and functions that characterize a product, service, or result." To clarify what this means let's look at Exhibit 3.1.

The column on the left contains a selection of project management items that need to be completed on the project. The column on the right contains a selection of technical items that need to be completed on the product. Project scope addresses those items on the left side of the table, and product scope addresses those on the right side. Attention is often focused on the right side because that's the reason that you are doing the project. However, it's very difficult to complete the items on the right without doing at least some of the items on the left. Years ago, when projects were functional in nature (an engineer leading an engineering project using engineering resources to produce an engineering product), it wasn't bad to have a technical project manager. But in today's complex product environment, project managers often become technical generalists and project experts (leaders). When this is the case, they rely on the project team members to support them with technical issues. Of course the project manager needs to be aware of some of the technical requirements and, even on smaller projects, may choose to have a technical lead on the project. When projects start to fall behind schedule or run over budget, the focus shifts to the right side when, in fact, the focus should be concentrated on the left side. A non-technical project manager with good general management skills will keep the focus where it's most needed rather than getting bogged down in the technical details.

The Project Scope Statement

During the initiation process the sponsor or another executive has defined, at a very high level, the project in the project charter. During planning much more information is available, and the team then further defines the project's deliverables as well as the work that's required to create those deliverables. This information becomes the project scope statement. The project scope statement is a living document that often determines how well the project management team can control the overall project scope. In other words, referring back to Exhibit 3.1, the scope statement entails both sides of the table. The scope statement is defined in the *PMBOK®* *Guide* and includes the following:

- The product scope description progressively elaborates the characteristics of the product, service, or result that the project was undertaken to create. It will typically contain less detail in the earlier project phases than in the later phases. The information for the product scope description is derived from the project charter and from any requirements documentation.

- Deliverables include the outputs and tangible results of the product or service as well as other items such as reports or documentation. Depending on the project, these deliverables can be described in detail or at a higher level.

◆ The acceptance criteria define the process and criteria that will be used to determine if the end product is acceptable.

◆ Project exclusions identify what is to be excluded from the project. Often project managers will say, "Why? If it isn't included in the project deliverables, then it isn't a part of the project!" Unfortunately, customers and other stakeholders often have different interpretations of what the project deliverables include. Stating specifically what's excluded from the project will help to manage stakeholder expectations and prevent problems down the road.

◆ Other elements may also be included in the scope statement. Other possible inclusions could be:

◆ Constraints list what will limit the team's options. Constraints are the "thou shalts" on the project such as "Thou shalt start the project on June 1" or "Thou shalt complete this project within this budget." Usually, a number such as a date or a cost should be listed as a constraint.

◆ Assumptions list the items that the team considers to be real, true, and certain. Assumptions allow the team to move forward. For example, an assumption may be that the team will have an adequate amount of resources to do the project or that funding will be available as needed. It's critical to understand that if assumptions are made, and they probably should be, then it's key to frequently validate those assumptions. If assumptions allow you to move forward on the project, keep in mind that you don't want to go too far down the "project road" without checking road signs along the way to make sure that you're still on the right road. Going too far without this validation may well lead to re-work, increased cost, falling behind on the schedule, and decreased quality.

◆ High-level risks can also be important particularly in development-type projects. High level risks are often identified as part of the project charter, but those risks are from the viewpoint of the key stakeholders. In the scope statement the risks are from the standpoint of the team. Just as in the project charter it is important not to do any type of analysis on the risks but simply to list them.

Exhibit 3-2. The Triple Constraint

Developing the Project Management Plan and Project Documents

The project management plan is a living document that includes everything that's needed to define, integrate, and coordinate all the plans in one place. It defines how the project will be managed, monitored, and controlled. The size and complexity of the project will determine how extensive the project management plan needs to be. Just a few examples of the subsidiary plans that are included in the project management plan are the project scope management plan, schedule management plan, cost management plan, risk management plan, and communications plan. The project management plan is maintained in the project repository. It's important to differentiate the project management plan from the project documents. The project management plan consists of all of the subsidiary plans, but the project documents are change logs, lessons learned register, project calendars, etc. Both reside in the project repository, usually part of the project management information system (PMIS).

The Triple Constraint and Project Planning

Exhibit 3.2 illustrates the balancing act that's at the heart of project planning: the triple constraint. The equilateral triangle has three equal sides of *schedule, cost,* and *scope.* In the center of the triangle is quality, implying that quality has an impact on, and is impacted by, all three elements of the

CUSTOMER PRIORITY MATRIX			
	Higher Priority	Lower Priority	Why? (Impact on quality, business value, other)
Scope	X		
Schedule	X		
Cost		X	

Exhibit 3-3. Customer Priority Matrix
This tool is used to help determine a customer's priorities.

triple constraint. Although the triple constraint is no longer in the *PM-BOK® Guide,* it still remains the basis of project management. The bottom line is that if you make a change to one side of the triangle you need to evaluate the impact on the other two sides of the triangle.

Picture a three-legged stool. One day you notice that it seems crooked. Wanting to even it out, you shave off a little from one or two of the legs, but then it's even more crooked. You continually shave a little off the legs, trying to make it even. Now imagine that an egg is on the seat. The egg represents quality. As you shave off the legs, sometimes the egg rolls to one side, then to another. If you don't get the stool even, the egg falls off. That's exactly what happens on projects. If the project is too far off the plan, quality may be sacrificed. Saving money by not hiring resources may mean that the schedule goes long; adding resources to speed things up bloats the budget. Out of the imperatives "better, faster, cheaper," it's really only possible to choose two. Prudent management usually consists of balancing schedule, cost, and scope.

The Priority Matrix

The priority matrix is a tool that project managers can use to determine what their customer's top priority is: cost, schedule, or scope (see Exhibit 3.3). You can add other items such as quality or security, but it's best not to consider more than five items. The trick to using this tool is to ask the right questions. For example, if you ask the customer "What's the highest priority among these three items?" the customer is probably going to answer,

"All of them!" Therefore you have to be more specific. Begin by explaining that you'll do your best to meet all the requirements within the time allocated and with the given budget, but sometimes things happen on a project. Ask questions such as, "If, once underway with this high-risk project, we find that we need more money to cover risk contingencies, would that be OK?" Or you can say, "Why is this completion date important to you?" By asking specific, open-ended questions you get a much better picture of what's important to the customer. Since customer satisfaction is an important criterion, it makes sense to be clear about the customer's priorities. If the project begins to fall behind and the customer has said that schedule is most important, then you may need to spend money on additional resources to get the project back on schedule.

The Work Breakdown Structure

Organizing the work properly, so that all the deliverables are identified, estimated, and scheduled, will lead to better project execution. The WBS is a key tool for ensuring project success. It should be produced immediately after the scope statement. The *PMBOK® Guide* glossary defines the WBS as "a hierarchical decomposition of the total scope of work to be carried out by the project team to accomplish the project objectives and create the required deliverables." Most importantly, the WBS is the primary tool that provides the project team and the customer with a comprehensive view of the project's scope, and it becomes the basis for the tracking system. Working as a team to develop the WBS increases team commitment to project deliverables. And it helps to provide the dual vision that team members need – not only to see what each member must do to complete his or her tasks on the project but also to see how each person's role fits into the overall project.

By using the project scope statement, the project team can begin with the big picture and make sure that the deliverables listed on the project scope statement are included in the WBS.

In a predictive-type project (a traditional project that's usually repetitive) it's fairly easy to define the WBS up front. In the adaptive/agile approach the WBS is developed as the project progresses. Whatever the type

0.0 Aircraft Servicing (project deliverable)

1.0 Service

  1.1 Fuel

  1.2 Food/drink

    1.2.1 1st class (work package)

    1.2.2 Coach (work package)

  1.3 Cleaning

  1.4 Maintenance

2.0 Passengers

  2.1 Unload

    2.1.1 Regular (work package)

    2.1.2 Special Needs (work package)

  2.2 Load

    2.2.1 1st class (work package)

    2.2.2 Coach (work package)

    2.2.3 Special Needs (work package)

Exhibit 3.4. Work Breakdown Structure in Outline Format

of project, the major deliverables must be defined in the project charter and the scope statement.

There are two formats for the WBS: outline or hierarchical. The hierarchical format looks very much like an organizational chart; the outline format is shown in Exhibit 3.4. Interestingly enough, in many software packages today the WBS is shown in the outline format, yet when most people think of creating a WBS, they visualize the hierarchical format, and this is in our view the best format to use when developing a WBS in a team setting. Common terminology for the top level is *project deliverable*, while the lowest level is called the *work package*.

Whichever format is used there are typically three approaches:

1. **Product approach:** This approach starts with the project deliverable. The second level lists the major deliverables. Each major deliverable is then further decomposed.

2. **Phased approach:** Again the approach begins with the project deliverable at the top. The second level of decomposition lists the project phases. The decomposition would then break down the deliverables to be completed in each phase.

3. **Functional approach:** The top level remains as the project deliverable. The second level lists the functions that will be assuming responsibility. The decomposition then defines the deliverables for each function

To illustrate this concept, let's look at how a WBS can be applied to a project. For this example we'll be using the phased approach. If you will, visualize that it's a spectacular Sunday afternoon in your hometown. You decide to take your significant other and your small child out for a drive to enjoy the beautiful day. As you're driving along the small child sits contentedly in the car seat, staring out the window.

All is right with the world until suddenly, dead ahead, you see the familiar logo of a popular fast-food restaurant, and from the back seat comes a screech, "I want a Tyke Treat Meal right now, please!" Two of the key stakeholders in the car, you and your significant other, decide that you're willing to take on this mini-project that we'll call "purchasing and consuming a children's fast-food meal" or "Tyke Treat Meal" for short.

So you pull into the parking lot, get out of the car, take the small child by the hand, and proceed into the restaurant. You state to the new stakeholder behind the counter the objective that has been so clear to all of the stakeholders in the vehicle: "I want a Tyke Treat right now, please!" The new stakeholder isn't quite as clear however and asks a question: "What kind of a Tyke Treat?" At this point, you can say that your project objective is the Tyke Treat, and further clarification of this project deliverable is acceptable and normal as the project proceeds. If, however, the child now says, "I've changed my mind, I want to go to Burger Heaven," then the project deliverable has changed and you would have a new project. Remember that the project deliverable is the top level of the WBS.

In this case, however, the child wants a Cheeseburger Tyke Treat; thus all of the stakeholders should now be clear on what the child (the customer) wants.

But the new stakeholder comes back with another question. "What kind of drink do you want?" Again, further clarification is acceptable and normal. Once you respond with: "I want a Cheeseburger Tyke Treat with a cola, please," there may be even more questions, and once those questions have been answered, you pay for and receive your project deliverable, the Tyke Treat.

You want to ensure that your customer is satisfied, since customer satisfaction helps to define a successful project, so you want to verify that all of the contents have been delivered. Do you have a defect? If not, the child will consume the Tyke Treat, and then you'll depart the restaurant and your project will conclude.

If you began to construct the WBS in the hierarchical format, you would have the project level as "Tyke Treat Meal." The second level of major deliverables will be:

- Arrival
- Purchase Verification
- Dining
- Departure

You will further decompose each major deliverable and have a WBS that looks something like Exhibit 3-5.

The elements under each major deliverable that have not been further broken down become two work packages. "Parking Lot and Restaurant" under the major deliverable of "Arrival" has not been broken down. If you decide formally that you don't want to break down French fries into work packages then French fries itself would become the work package and all the sub-elements would be eliminated. The work packages will shift as the project proceeds (and more detailed breakdown of the work occurs), which is one reason that the WBS is considered to be a living document.

As you do your validation, you should check to make sure that, if you complete all of the work, you will have completed the project objective

0 Tyke Treat Meal

1 Arrival	2 Purchase	3 Verification & Validation	4 Dining	5 Departure
1.1 Parking lot	2.1 Order	3.1 Validation of contents	4.1 Consumption	5.1 Trash disposal
1.2 Restaurant	2.2.1 Tyke Treat	3.1.1 Cheesburger	4.1.1 Cheesburger	5.2 Restaurant departure
	2.2.2 Cola	3.1.1.1 Meat	4.1.2 French fries	
	2.2.3 Selection of toy	3.1.1.2 Cheese	4.1.3 Cola	
	2.3 Client confirmation of contents	3.1.1.3 Bun	4.2 Cleanup	
	2.4 Order confirmation	3.1.1.4 Condiments		
	2.5 Payment	3.1.1.4.1 Pickles		
	2.6 Receipt of Tyke Treat meal	3.1.1.4.2 Onions		
		3.1.1.4.3 Ketchup		
		3.2.1.5.2 Mustard		
		3.1.2 French fries		
		3.1.2.1 Grease		
		3.1.2.2 Salt		
		3.1.2.3 Potatoes		
		3.1.3 Cola		
		3.1.3.1 Cup		
		3.1.3.1 Straw		
		3.1.3.1 Lid		
		3.1.3.1 Liquid		

Exhibit 3-5. Work Breakdown Structure Decomposed

of "purchasing and consuming a Cheeseburger Tyke Treat." Remarkably, sometimes when you go through this validation of the WBS, you'll find that some critical piece of work has been omitted. Now is the time to catch those omissions so that you minimize the need for changes later in the project (along with their attendant schedule delays and cost overruns).

Team participation in building the WBS increases commitment and communication and reduces the chance of omitting any of the needed work. The WBS details costs for equipment, labor, and material for each element within it. Because each element is a measurable unit of work, the WBS can become a basis for monitoring progress against the baseline for both cost and schedule.

Remember that the WBS is intended to be helpful in managing the project; therefore, consideration should be given to how the project will gather and report status. Structure the WBS to help make that happen. Be thorough, but don't succumb to analysis paralysis. If the team gets into identifying work packages that require as little as eight to ten hours, they will increase the management time needed to track them. Limit the level of detail of the WBS to whatever will help manage the project.

The numbering system translates into an effective cost-tracking system. One example of a numbering system would place the project level at 0.0; the three major deliverables beneath would be 1.0, 2.0, 3.0. Under the 1.0 would be 1.1, 1.2, and so on, as illustrated in Exhibit 3-5. Resources, costs, and time are assigned at the work package level.

The Resource Assignment Matrix

In order to be able to manage the resource data in the WBS, you'll need to create a resource assignment matrix (RAM) like the example in Exhibit 3.6. This document helps detail the ownership of each work package and the amount of effort required of each resource on that work. The RAM is created by listing each work package in the project (usually by its identifying number) along the left hand vertical axis of the matrix and each job position that will be used on the project across the top horizontal axis. The matrix is quadrille-ruled and can either be left as squares or each

RESOURCE ASSIGNMENT MATRIX				
Resource Work package	Driver	Passenger	Customer	Counter Person
2.1 Order Tyke Treat	P	S		
2.2 Answer questions	P	S	S	
2.3 Confirm order	S		P	S
2.4 Pay for Tyke Treat	P	S		

Exhibit 3-6. Resource Assignment Matrix: Tyke Treat Meal
The resource assignment matrix for our project, Tyke Treat Meal, shows who is responsible for various work packages (noted with a "P") and who has a supporting role (noted with an "S").

square split at a 45 degree angle. Where the squares are maintained, the data entered in the blocks is normally limited to who will have primary responsibility for the work package (noted with a "P") and who will have a supporting role (noted by an "S"). If the split square format is used, in addition to the "P" or "S" being entered in the first half of the square, the number of effort hours anticipated for that person on the specific work package is entered. This combination of information becomes especially valuable both for overall estimating of effort hours for each person, for each work package, and, in scheduling, for resource allocation, and earlier recognition of resource conflicts between work packages scheduled to run at the same time.

Developing the Project Schedule

Schedule development is discussed in detail in chapter 5, but for the purposes of planning it's important to remember that a schedule is, at best, the planned sequence of events. The schedule has several views, but they all serve to measure progress against time.

The value of the schedule is that it serves to measure the team's progress on a number of levels. The variance analysis that comes from the schedule allows for better decision making within the boundaries of your "panic parameters." Using software to manage the schedule also allows for numerous "what if" analyses. This leads to better strategic and tactical decision making.

A Planning Reality – The Rolling Wave

The reality of project management planning is that you seldom know and can't foresee all of the issues and risks in a project. This is particularly true of adaptive/agile projects. As you move through the project, however, more information becomes available. This concept is encapsulated in the rolling-wave planning theory, which explains that at the beginning of the first phase of a project your knowledge of that project is at its lowest point. As you move through each phase, your knowledge of the phase grows to a wave crest, then, as you begin the next phase your knowledge falls down into a trough, but after each phase the trough is not as deep as the preceding trough. So the wave tops are getting higher in total amplitude, but the base level is also rising. This represents the increasing knowledge of the project that the project team has developed. So it's not uncommon to know very little about the project when you begin, but with time and experience you'll become very knowledgeable. Therefore, when planning a project it's invaluable to contact others who have done similar projects in the past, since they often can add important insights and help you do better planning. This information gathering can be done in person, by reviewing prior project files, and by reviewing lessons learned. However you do it, it's an essential part of planning.

Planning, when well done, sets the project up for success; and, conversely, poor planning is the most common cause of project failure. So plan on success!

CHAPTER FOUR

Project Cost and Budget

WHY DEFINE AND TRACK project cost and budget? Without the right information at the right time, project managers and teams often act when they shouldn't, and fail to act when they should. Simply stated, if you don't know where you planned to be, then wherever you are means nothing because it lacks context: all variation is equal and lots of corrective action usually winds up being required. If this sounds familiar, then you probably find yourself in chaos far too often. Chaos usually exists in the uncontrolled state. The most common and challenging causes of chaos for project managers are non-linear, dynamic events, such as scope changes or risk events, which occur on *all* projects but in unpredictable ways or at unpredictable times. How do you effectively manage in such a chaotic environment? By establishing and employing sound cost estimating and budgeting methods.

An important first step toward order is to begin with clarity around project expectations. In project management language, this is your "area of order" and is a key part of the project baseline. According to the *PMBOK*® *Guide,* the baseline is "the approved version of a work product that can be changed only through formal change control procedures and is used as a basis for comparison to actual results." Two keys of this definition are that the baseline is "approved" by some authority (sponsor, customer, etc.) and stands as an agreement and expectation for the project. Also, the phrase "can be changed only through formal change control procedures" suggests that this baseline is a "living" document. The baseline should always represent the current approved plan for its respective project. Project teams use their baseline as they gather project results, analyze the data, and decide if corrective or enhancement actions are necessary. The elements included in the project baseline vary from organization to organization as project oversight teams (portfolio management teams, strategic investment teams, program teams) define which factors they want included. Once defined and implemented, these factors help to ensure that a consistent review of projects is possible, status is understood, and key support actions are taken as appropriate.

One of the areas that many project leadership teams and project managers agree should be included in the baseline is cost. The cost of a project results from the calculation of the costs of each of the work items, which are then aggregated to higher summary levels until ultimately the entire project has its cost defined. Once this aggregated cost has been approved and assigned to the project, it then becomes a key part of the project's actual budget (material and other costs will be added to complete the budget). The project budget is the financial summation and foundation of the project cost or spend plan. The budget is frequently established in stages – the proposed budget, the initial budget, and, once negotiated and approved, the project baseline budget. As costs are expensed from the budget they're termed *expensed budget items*.

Ideally a good estimating process would precede the budget. But, regrettably, in too many cases the budget precedes an effective estimate. Some reasons that organizations give for doing this are:

- ◆ They spend too much time defining costs for opportunities they don't win, which is wasteful.

- ◆ They don't have the resources to do it.

- ◆ They don't know enough about the project.

- ◆ They wanted to estimate first, before budgeting, but needed to value-price the outcome (lower the bid to win).

All of these might be occasional reasons for developing a budget prior to having good estimates, but when it becomes the unquestioned routine, it creates real problems. Too many organizations take shortcuts to their budget number without good reasons. If your organization is losing money on projects, leadership may want to look at its project costing and baseline budgeting processes as potential areas for improvement. Without an effective cost baseline and budget you're challenged in your ability to manage and control the project. If a project manager reports to his or her program manager, "I have completed 85 percent of my work," the effective program manager would need more information – a broader view of performance to balance that performance result against other critical project factors in order to really understand the current performance. That program manager should wonder, "How much have I paid for this work?" "Was overtime involved?" "How much was planned to be accomplished at this point in time?" The project cost baseline helps you to understand how much things really cost by allowing you to:

◆ Establish the cost for each of the project's work items before authorizing implementation.

◆ Track project performance (for both in-house and contracted resources) against those planned costs.

◆ Identify and analyze variance.

As you can see, there are lots of benefits to defining and managing project costs. So why don't more organizations make it an established practice? Some of the reasons frequently given:

◆ It takes too much time.

◆ It's unnecessary bureaucracy.

◆ We don't know how to do it.

◆ We lack the internal system capability to do it.

◆ It slows us down.

◆ If management knew how much these things really cost, we would lose our jobs!

Though many of these "reasons" may be real, they aren't insurmountable. Collecting cost data helps the current project succeed, and if data is retained and examined it can be used to help improve project performance. Another key reason in support of using consistent approaches to cost management in today's downsized, economically sensitive environment is that project managers are increasingly expected to lead more and more projects at the same time. Additionally, project team members are supporting several different projects at the same time, and if each of these projects requires team members to use different tools and approaches, then inefficiency and chaos will result at every level of the organization.

Key Cost and Budget Terms

Real improvement is built on a foundation of knowledge derived from standardization so that project successes are repeatable. One of the key areas for standardization is language. Here are some key terms associated with project cost and budget.

Costs

A cost is an assigned quantitative value (usually monetary) assigned to a resource that is planned to be expended or has been expended to achieve the project's product, service, or result. This definition makes it clear that cost is a basic consideration in defining and managing a project. In most cases costs are calculated iteratively: that is, as more and more of the project details become known, the cost estimate will change. In those cases where the project may be long term or complex and, initially, many of the details of the project are not clearly defined yet, it may be wise to estimate the cost of just the first phase of the project. Based upon that result, you can more effectively estimate the next phase. This approach is known as rolling-wave estimating.

Cost Objects

Cost objects are the items for which cost is being assessed in estimating or calculating project cost. In project management the cost object is typically

MATERIALS	HUMAN RESOURCES
✓ Hardware	✓ Customer resource costs
✓ Software	• Business partner costs
✓ Supplies	• Supplier estimates and costs
✓ Facilities (rental, construct)	✓ Technical support
✓ Tools	• Subject matter experts
✓ Special equipment	• Other consultants
✓ Travel	✓ Labor
✓ Shipping	• Overhead
✓ Verification and validation testing	• Annual salary increases

Exhibit 4-1. Types of Direct Costs

the work package (see chapter 3). Those who try to estimate a project's cost by using the whole project, without detail, as the cost object miss the point and in most cases, the resultant estimate will be widely inaccurate.

Direct Costs

Direct costs are any costs that can be traced to a unique project element or committed cost object. The project team should establish the baseline direct costs, re-establish them with approved changes, and track project performance against this baseline. In tracking direct costs, the project team will establish Control Accounts (CAs) and may employ Control Account Managers (CAMs) to establish a Control Account Plan (CAP) to ensure that each project cost has a unique identifier and is tracked and controlled effectively. Exhibit 4-1 lists some typical direct costs.

Indirect Costs

Indirect costs are not assigned to a specific project but are accumulated and allocated equitably over multiple projects by some approved and documented accounting procedure. An example might be inventory costs that are accrued at the program level but are divided among all the projects within that program. These costs can be frustrating to a project manager, who is trying to closely manage project cost elements to enable better profitability or productivity, if he or she is in an organization in which the indirect costs are arbitrarily assigned. Great project results can be made to look bad in an organization in which the indirect costs are applied arbitrarily or inequitably. Every project manager should know the origin and basis of costs that affect their project. Overhead costs; contributions to the corporation; and sales, general, and administrative (SG&A) costs are some of the more common indirect project cost objects.

Fixed Costs

Fixed costs are project costs that are planned to remain constant. For example, if a project needs a machine to do drilling work, and it's rented at $400 a week, that's a fixed cost for each week the machine is used. A caution when dealing with fixed costs is to watch out for changes resulting from valid variation such as inflation, increases in negotiated labor rates, fluctuation in the value of the dollar, changes required as a result of new accounting rules each year, or other factors.

Variable Costs

Variable costs are costs that will or may vary over the life of the project based upon various usage scenarios. Typically, the various rates and scenarios will be defined as part of the arranged cost of the object. An example of a variable cost would be the cost of project electricity. The base rate of the electricity will remain constant, but the cost will vary based upon the number of kilowatt hours used. Note that it's possible to have both fixed and variable direct costs and indirect costs.

Effort

Effort is the number of labor units required to complete a schedule activity or WBS component (PMI 2017, p. 705). If you sum up all the hours of effort you'll have the total hours of required work on the project. Effort can be expressed as labor units, people hours, hours, days, or weeks.

Duration

Duration is the total number of work periods consumed by the effort (not including holidays or other nonworking periods) to complete a scheduled activity or WBS component. With most project management software, the project manager establishes the work hours and the work days. Duration is normally expressed in a manner that represents the impact against the work calendar, such as "work weeks" or "one staff day."

Calendar Time

Calendar time (also known as elapsed time) is the actual calendar days or hours, including weekends, consumed by the effort and not just the time defined by the work period. For example; a project has a 40-hour task and works a planned 8-hour work day. This task has a planned 5-day duration (40 hours / 5). However, if the task begins Thursday morning, a 5-day duration will complete at the end of the day the following Wednesday. This one task is 40 hours of effort, 5 days of duration and 7 days of calendar time (because calendar time or elapsed time counts non-work days such as Saturday and Sunday). This may add unexpected time to the project plan and bloat the result.

In working with effort and duration, the project manager needs to recognize the nuances of each element and how each might affect project cost and work performance. If a task is defined as having a fixed duration of one day (the default is eight hours), it doesn't matter how many resources are assigned – it will still take one work day. If a task is not a fixed-duration task, and it's a one-day duration task (eight hours of effort), then the addition of a second resource may be an effective way of reducing the duration to a half day. However, the effort required will still be eight hours, or it may even increase slightly. The addition of one resource to this eight-hour task will not always cut it to four hours, because it's seldom a direct linear reduction.

Price

Price is a monetary value assigned to sell or market a product, service, or result. Sometimes there's a real disconnect between cost and price. The cost may be determined to be $1 million, and with a targeted 30 percent profit, the price should be $1,300,000 (cost + profit = price). However, for many reasons, such as fear of losing the contract, a lower price is given.

In order to recover from this low bid, the hope is to be able to regain that profit margin by adding change or extra work or scope to the project. Are there reasons a contract may be lower than desired? Yes. It may be that the contractor hopes to get a foot in the door and make up the low contract price by developing an ongoing relationship with the client. The hope is that profit will result from the long-term relationship. The law of supply and demand also plays a role in setting the final price. If, for example, you're the only makers of a product that's in high demand, you can set the price rather high. Once competitors come into the marketplace, you shift to a competitive pricing model, which typically lowers the price. Project managers need to understand the concept of pricing because there are steps that they can take to enhance profitability if they know their costs and their pricing. For example, a project manager who is managing four projects, all requiring the same base material provided by an external vendor, can, once the cost baseline and price of the project are set, approach the vendor for volume discounts or to see about bundling other services in order to lower costs.

Profit

Profit is simply the incoming revenues for the project minus the costs to produce it.

Cost Estimating Methods

The goal of any estimator should be to employ the method that provides the most efficient but accurate estimate. Sounds simple enough, but it's a challenge because accuracy is often sacrificed for expediency and, once established, the estimate isn't updated as more information becomes known. The lack of a process to update our estimates is a particular problem because it's well known that any system (especially project estimates), once it's established, doesn't maintain its level of excellence unless it's continuously updated and improved. Project managers and estimators must embrace the idea of *iterative approximation*. Iterative approximation is the recognition that any estimate has its limitations because project events are dynamic and require continuous updating.

COST ESTIMATING METHODS	
✓ Expert judgment	✓ Reserve analysis
✓ Parametric/top-down estimating	✓ Cost of quality
✓ Definitive/bottom-up estimating	✓ Analogous estimating
✓ Vendor bid analysis	✓ Computer-generated estimating
✓ Pull it directly out of midair estimating	✓ PERT (program evaluation and review technique) or three-point estimating

Exhibit 4-2. Cost Estimating Methods

The most common project cost estimates usually fall into two general categories: top-down or bottom-up. These are used at different points in the project life cycle because of the amount of data or detail available. Exhibit 4.2 lists various estimating methods.

Top-Down Estimates

Top-down estimating starts with understanding the project goal and final deliverables (the first level of the WBS) and then breaking the WBS down into smaller planning chunks. There isn't a lot of detail at the lowest levels in this approach, but the biggest pieces are clear and estimated. This approach works well when the project manager and the team know the project very well. A variant, and maybe least effective application of the top-down approach is the order of magnitude (also known as the rough order of magnitude (ROM) approach. This estimate uses historical data or experiential data from similar projects, and it's used when little or no information is known about a project. Practitioners have many names for this approach – rough order of magnitude and vague approximation are two of them – and this is often the estimate that gets into project nomination documentation. These up-front early estimates may have a range of accuracy of -25% to +75%.

Bottom-Up Estimates

The definitive or bottom-up estimate uses each work package or lowest-level activity of the WBS or similar tool as the basis for the estimate. It's an approach to determine the cost of the project cost objects. All these costs are aggregated into an overall summary cost for different levels of the project. Normally this approach is more accurate (-5% to +10%) than top-down estimating.

Estimating Tools/Techniques

Expert Judgment

In some cases where formal historical data doesn't exist, the judgment of subject matter experts (SMEs) or subject matter groups (SMGs) can be used to develop or validate an estimate. Be sure to be open to data from a broad range of sources including industry data, diverse non-typical groups of experts, and any other source for expert insight that might be overlooked if we go to the same source all the time. Also ensure that data elements are adjusted for time and other factors.

Analogous (Analogy) Estimate

This estimating approach calculates a project's cost or duration using historical or experiential data from a previous, similar project. This approach is popular because it's easy and fast, but you must use caution to ensure that the reference project *is* similar and the data *is still valid* for the current time.

Parametric Estimate

The parametric approach uses an algorithm to calculate cost or duration based on historical data and project parameters (PMI 2017, p. 712). For example: A state engages a road construction company to build some roads. The planned roads are straight and must extend for 10 miles. The road company tells the state, "Our price is $100,000 per straight mile of road. You want 10 miles, so the price is $10 \times \$100,000 = \$1$ million."

Program Evaluation and Review Technique or Three-Point Estimates

In some cases, project work may be so complex or risky that it's difficult to estimate. A popular approach for including risk in your estimate is to use

A project manager is trying to determine duration (in days) of a particular task in order to estimate the cost. This task has not been performed by this organization before. The task performers estimate that they can perform the work in 15 days (ML). Also, a team of subject matter experts assessing the potential risks determined that if all went badly, the task could take 40 days (P). Those same experts also determined that if all went smoothly the task could be completed in as little as 8 days (O). Using the formula for calculating the PERT estimate, the result is as follows:

$$(40 + 60 + 8) \div 6 = \text{a PERT estimate of 18 days}$$

This suggests that the project manager should consider scheduling the task for 18 days instead of 15 (the most likely), and that will allow for some risk. This concept can also be applied to series of tasks, whole sub-projects, and whole projects. This functionality is also built into many of today's project management software tools.

Exhibit 4-3. Example of a PERT Estimate

the three-point estimating approach or PERT estimate. This approach can be used for estimating project time or project cost. The approach includes:

◆ Most Likely (ML): The result that the SME or performer believes is the typical result.

◆ Optimistic (O): The result if all goes exactly according to plan.

◆ Pessimistic (P): The result if all goes contrary to plan.

The PERT formula is:

$$\text{ESTIMATE} = (P + 4 \times ML + O) \div 6$$

See Exhibit 4-3 for an example of a PERT estimate.

Data Analysis Estimating

Sometimes when estimating, it's helpful to examine data from prior performances or data from other sources. Some of those sources might be:

Alternatives Analysis
(also known as "what if" estimating and analysis)

Cost-estimating decisions will normally have several possible alternatives. These alternatives and their attendant data should be evaluated to make the best costing decision. For example, in retail projects you can gather customer response and feedback to your new product by doing in-store testing *or* you can do simple baseline studies of industry data *or* you can do an in-house focus group, etc. Each of these approaches has a different cost, a different time, a different validity, etc. All the data for each alternative must be studied and compared to objectives, and a decision should be made based upon that analysis.

Reserve Analysis

Project managers will frequently add additional funds to an estimate to be held in reserve in case unexpected events occur during the project life cycle. In many cases, there's a set percentage of the overall project cost estimate (10% to 15%), and this is applied after the estimate has been developed. Additionally, reviewing the contingency reserve consumption data from prior projects may give insight into how an estimate might need to be adjusted up or down.

Cost of Quality

The desired level of quality will impact the cost estimate as well. Knowing the data for expected quality performance and using that data when developing or adjusting your estimate can be a good practice. The cost-of-quality concept identifies major categories of cost in a project. Those costs are the *cost of conformance* and the *cost of nonconformance*. Simply stated, the concept is that if you can do a great job at planning quality in (conformance costs) you will limit and reduce the costs of nonconformance (defects or other problems). The benefit of this knowledge is that your cost-of-quality data from previous projects are recorded for historical records and analyzed for knowledge that can be used to estimate future project results, thus making your project estimates more reliable.

Pulled It Directly Out of Mid-Air
(PIDOOMA) Estimate

This estimate isn't based on any of the details of the project or historical record or previous experience. It's just a guess, and regrettably it's used too often in place of a real estimate. It should be treated as the opposite of the firm quote, but it often isn't. In many cases, once spoken, the PIDOOMA bid is firm. This type of bid also has other names such as:

◆ SWAG – sales went ahead and guessed

◆ GWOP – goals without planning

◆ PURGE – precise unrealistic guesstimate

These terms are offered as evidence that you don't have to lose your sense of humor when you become a project manager.

Computer-Generated Estimates
(Software Estimating)

Today's computer-based project management information system (PMIS) can be a key tool when estimating and costing. These tools enable project managers to be both fast and more accurate in their estimates. Computer-supported cost management is especially helpful for large and complex projects. For smaller, less-complex projects many of the general-purpose spreadsheets such as Microsoft Excel or Lotus 1-2-3 are suitable. It's important to note that if you're managing several projects, or if you're a program manager leading several projects within your program, it may be important to use the same cost management system for all of your projects. This will help you to roll up costs effectively. Without standardization you'll receive information that you can't use because it's been created in different ways.

Problems with Estimates and Estimating

There are some frequent and challenging causes of inaccuracy in cost and time estimates attributable to a great many sources – lack of experience, organizational culture, ineffective or non-existent project support processes (e.g. risk processes, resource processes), and a climate of fear.

- **Inexperienced planners.** Inexperienced planners are a major problem for projects. The person assigned often doesn't have experience with this specific type of work or may not have estimating experience, and therefore the estimate they offer is inaccurate.

- **Non-committed resources.** In this scenario the person offering the estimate doesn't have to perform the work. Therefore, he or she has no commitment to its quality or accomplishment. Often when functional managers contribute data to the project, they don't have manuals or historical records to use in deriving the estimate, and therefore they provide their best guess. That estimate is often based on how long the experienced manager might take to perform that task (optimistic). Yet when it comes time on the project to perform that task, it's performed by an assigned worker who in many cases lacks the skill and expertise of the functional manager and has no commitment to the estimate, and thus will often not achieve that optimistic estimate.

- **Fear.** In organizations with a lot of fear (instead of trust) between management and project personnel, estimates become inflated, the estimating process is circumvented, and padding occurs. Fear is caused by many factors including: competitive pressures, poor project manager relationship skills, ineffective organizational leadership behaviors, and punitive reward and recognition systems. Fear manifests itself in many ways, and it can be a major cause of troubled projects. Here are two examples:

  - One organization used a color coding system – red for problems needing immediate attention, yellow for emerging problems, and green for "no major issues, proceed with plan." As the program team reviewed cost results, they noticed that most of the items were green, approximately 25 percent were red, and *none* were yellow. They reviewed previous data and realized that in most cases only green and red

DOCUMENTS TO REVIEW BEFORE ESTIMATING THE PROJECT	
✓ Contract	✓ Standards
✓ Project charter	✓ Key dates
✓ Estimating manuals	✓ Scope documents
✓ Resource lists	✓ Letters of agreement
✓ Resource costs	✓ Documents of understanding
✓ Organization rules	

Exhibit 4-4. Estimator's Checklist

were used to report status. They eventually realized that the manager in this area became so angry when receiving bad news that project managers covered up negative data until it could no longer be ignored and had to be reported as *red*. By this time, of course, the cost of correcting problems was much higher.

- Another example of fear is the project manager who constantly increases the cost estimate 10 to 20 percent because they fear that their manager will reduce that estimate. It's also true that when project managers constantly reduce cost estimates this causes subordinates to increase their estimates. The net effect of six or seven project team members each increasing an estimate to allow for a manager's arbitrary cuts is a lot of unnecessary cost added to the project!

◆ **Lack of adequate information.** Making effective decisions requires sufficient information. Clearly the more information the project team has, the better able they are to create an accurate and complete estimate. Exhibit 4-4 suggests some (but not all) of the documents a project team should review prior to creating the estimate.

◆ **Uncertainty and risk.** Risk and uncertainty are a part of every project. That's to say that risk events will occur on your project, and to assume that they *won't* and fail to plan for them is a poor management practice. Of concern is the *impact* of risk events. The impact of risk and uncertainty increases as the project progresses, and a risk event that occurs late in the project life cycle can be far costlier than the cost to prevent it in the early stages of project work. Each project team should identify risk events, plan action to mitigate those risks, and include those actions in the cost estimate. In some cases, when action isn't necessary at the time, the project team will define and set aside some contingency funds. These funds should be added to the project estimate.

◆ **The cost of project management.** On some projects the cost of just managing the project could reach 20 percent or more of the total labor cost. Often this cost isn't included in the budget and therefore the real cost of executing projects isn't known. Your organization may decide that there should be a standard amount that will be applied to each project as a baseline cost for project management. In some cases, when the project you're executing is for an external organization, the customer may push back when the estimate or price includes project management costs. The customer in this case is being unrealistic, because every project has supervisory and management costs, and projects involving external customers often have higher costs in this area.

These are some of the factors that can shape the accuracy of your cost estimate – but they're not all the factors. Each project environment usually develops a set of tools and an approach to determine accurate estimates. An example of such tools is the Constructive Cost Model II (COCOMO® II) tool, which is an open-source tool used to estimate the effort and cost of software development projects. The project manager and project team should think deeply about the elements of their environment that may affect project cost.

The Cost and Budgeting Process

The project team can benefit from establishing a routine estimating process. The *PMBOK® Guide* suggests a cost management approach comprising four processes:

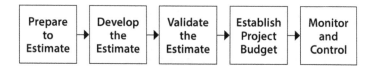

Exhibit 4-5. The Cost Estimating Process

- Plan cost management
- Estimate costs
- Determine budget
- Control costs

Exhibit 4-5 is an example of a generic cost estimating process.

Plan Cost Management

A key first step, plan cost management is the process of defining the characteristics of your project cost estimating process. In this process the project manager and project team define the policies, procedures, and documentation for planning, managing, expending, and controlling project costs. The project manager makes several decisions about how, when, and where the project team will develop the cost estimate. Some considerations are:

- What information will the team members or estimators need?
- What units of measurement will be used?
- What levels of accuracy, precision, and associated thresholds will be used?
- Which team members need to be in attendance?
- What tool will be used?
- What key roles will be used during the process?
- What process will be followed?
- Where will the estimating be done?

◆ When will the estimating be done?

◆ Will additional resources or support be required for this step in the process?

In preparing for planning cost management, the project team should review the following:

◆ Guidance information

• The project charter

• Scope information

◆ Enterprise environmental factors (relevant impact of markets, culture, currency, etc.)

◆ Organizational data and information (process assets) such as historical lessons learned, data bases, cost tool information, etc.

Estimate Costs

During this step the actual estimate or "approximation of the monetary resources needed to complete project work" is developed (PMI 2017, p. 231). It may be that a preliminary budget was defined for the project at its initiation, but that's *not necessarily* the budget (except in some contracted environments). As stated earlier, initial estimates, especially those known as rough order of magnitude (ROM) estimates, can have a wide range of accuracy. For that reason, it's necessary for the project team to apply their expertise to create an estimate to validate and update the ROM or estimate they were given. This may seem redundant, *but it's critical.* Often the budget was developed by individuals who don't have the in-depth knowledge that the project team members have. Additionally, this process of developing an estimate helps the team to:

◆ Determine the real cost of the project.

◆ Validate that the budget they were given is appropriate for this work.

◆ Become committed to the project through participation.

◆ Shape their thinking about timing, risk, and other project factors based upon the cost and resource decisions made in cost estimating.

◆ Gain a clearer understanding of the scope of the project.

The result of this process should be a project cost estimate that includes all the direct costs applicable for this project. You will then adjust that estimate to include the additional direct and indirect costs the team deems appropriate. This becomes your initial budget estimate. This estimate will change after other parts of the project plan are created. At this point you should begin to realize whether your assigned budget is adequate to meet project commitments. One of the problems with the practice of management by objectives (Drucker 1993) is that the objectives too often flow downhill without any opportunity for feedback. This process should overcome that deficiency. If the team can or chooses to do a full detailed bottom-up estimate, the range of accuracy can be -5% to + 10%. Two key added subprocesses that many teams execute are:

Validating the Estimate

Reflective learning and confirming are key activities that add to the accuracy of any estimate. When performing *reflective* activities the project team reviews their work to ensure that:

◆ Each assumption has been reviewed and, if possible, eliminated. Assumptions are factors that for planning purposes are true, real, or certain without proof or demonstration. Those assumptions that cannot be verified at this point in the project should be managed as risks, and those that you can validate should be treated as constraints in your estimate. Too many unverified or to-be-determined (TBD) assumptions are dangerous to your project cost result.

◆ The result will be consistent with published or mandated standards for this work.

◆ Risk has been included.

◆ Project management costs have been included.

Confirming the Estimate

When confirming the estimate, the project team reviews the estimate to validate that:

- Project goals can be achieved.

- The preliminary budget is still valid.

- Cost objects have been fairly assessed. In this case the team is trying to ensure that no function, skill, or equipment has been allocated funding that is too low or too high.

Determine Budget

If all the factors in the cost estimate seem correct, the next step usually is for the team to present their findings to project leadership or the customer for approval. This step may not follow immediately after validation. In some organizations there will be some intermediary activities that will occur that will affect your initial estimate. Project activities will have to be sequenced (discussed in chapter 5) and assigned dates. Those dates may affect cost – a long delay between activities may cause a contractor to raise costs, or a long delay may add travel costs. Other managerial actions and systems implemented, such as quality requirements, risk management, or change management, may add cost to the project as well.

In some cases, once all factors have been considered, your budget is higher than the contract or mandated budget. The project team should then review their budget with an eye toward taking out some of the fat (this is also called value engineering). Strategies to be considered might be:

- **De-scope or lessen the work to be accomplished on the project.** In many cases the project team knows from the start that they can't deliver all the scope requested in the timeframe or for the cost indicated. In order to reach the cost target, a practical consideration may be to reduce scope. Reducing scope is the actual removal or reduction of the features or functions of the product, service, or result to be delivered. This action must always be closely negotiated with all the key stakeholders. Additionally, the connectivity or interrelationship of this project to other projects within the program or organization should be considered.

◆ **Trim expenditures.** In this case, one of the project leaders (the project manager or the project sponsor) mandates an across-the-board or specific, targeted cost reduction. An example of this may be mandating a reduction in training expenses of 25 percent. When this strategy is employed it often obtains short-term benefits but may add costs in the long term. For example, you might obligate less money for training in the front of the project, but you might add costs as untrained personnel take longer to achieve goals.

◆ **Crash the work.** Crashing is the strategic application of additional resources to a specific task with the goal of reducing the total duration of that task. This may seem contradictory to our goal of cost reduction, but applying the right resources at the right point in time often will shorten duration and reduce costs. For example, a set of testing tasks is scheduled to last four weeks and cost $10,000 in labor. Discussions with the testing manager reveal that a contracting firm can provide an excellent resource at the cost of $2,220 a week (billable in whole weeks only), and that a skilled resource can accomplish the task in two weeks versus four. You decide to add that skilled resource to work with your resource, and as a result, the work is finished in one week and three days, at a cost of $8,445, and shaves two weeks and two days off the schedule! The project manager should try not to crash tasks currently in progress or tasks that are not on the critical path.

◆ **Defer expenditures.** On longer or larger projects, there may be some benefits from deferring expenditures. This is an example of the present-value approach. Most managers know that a dollar today is typically not worth as much at some point in the future. Some projects can benefit by closely managing their expenditures against their revenues. The rule is the longer you can delay spending project money the better, and the sooner you can get revenue the better.

◆ **Eliminate the fat.** This requires a detailed examination of project factors with an eye toward eliminating anything that doesn't add value to the customer. This can be subjective, and you must ensure that only non-value-added cost objects are removed from the project.

◆ **Improve productivity.** Some of the standard quality concepts and practices that emphasize doing it right the first time can be implemented, not merely as exhortation, but as real productive procedures that yield the desired efficiencies. This approach may require added time in the front of the project, but if done well it will save time in the later stages.

As you can see by the concepts and actions described above, project managers would do well to view their project budget as a key tool for strategy. Each budget should be examined for cost drivers, opportunities, and threats. The budget should be recognized as a constraint and managed accordingly. Effective project managers are successful at establishing an honest budget at the start of the project, updating it when there are approved changes, and managing it to its best result.

Presenting the Budget

Once it's been determined that the cost estimate is as accurate and effective as it can be, it should be presented to leadership for approval. The project now has a defined budget against which it will be executed, tracked, and controlled, unless it has an approved change.

Control Costs

Most project managers and project leaders recognize that there is variation in everything. Once the project plan is approved and the baseline is established, it's foolish to believe that the results will not vary. Quality reporter Lloyd Dobyns once said that "a system left unattended does not maintain its excellence; it begins immediately to degrade." That's certainly true in project management. The Control Cost process is about "monitoring the status of the project to update the project costs and manage changes to the cost baseline" (PMI 2017, p. 231). In some cases, the day you start executing the plan you're entering your first changes. A key tool for ensuring the desired result of the project is the approved project budget. The budget can function as a stand-alone tool for indicating where you should be at any point in time about cost and expenditures. Additionally, when the budget is used in conjunction with established systems such as earned value management, project monitoring and controlling is much more effective (see chapter 9).

ORGANIZATIONS SHOULD THINK deeply about their cost practices. Hope isn't a plan, and accurate cost and time estimates are foundational to your projects success. Concepts such as low-balling and underselling might win work, or make the boss happy, but at what cost to your organization's brand image, reputation, and profitability? If you cannot reliably deliver on time or on budget, then your long-term organizational health will suffer. A frequent source of debilitating project problems is the initial cost/price estimate – these problems can be avoided by taking a thoughtful and knowledgeable approach to your Project Cost Management.

CHAPTER FIVE

Scheduling the Project

magine planning an automobile trip to Florida, which is 400 miles away. Prior to the start of your trip you map out the route. As you're mapping you try to answer some key questions:

- What's the best, easiest route to get there?
- Where should I be at certain points in time?
- How long will this trip take?
- Are there any potential bottlenecks or other risky traffic areas to look out for?

The roadmap serves as your plan for the trip and is, once you finalize it, a prediction. An effective roadmap will enable you to answer those key questions that you have concerning the trip.

In project management the project schedule plays the same role. It's your roadmap to guide you and to help you manage activity and results. In some project environments, where most of the work is knowledge work, the schedule may be the only visual representation of the project deliverables that the team will have to manage and track their project. Like a roadmap, it predicts where you should be at key points in time and how long the trip (project) should last. It also helps to factor in the effects of trip dynamics such as traffic delays and weather, which are, in project management terms, the potential risks that may impact the schedule. An additional key aspect of a good schedule is that it will help you to analyze the impact of a change. For example, during your trip to Florida, you decide to visit friends 100 miles to the west of your planned route. With a good schedule you can assess the impact on the trip there, the trip back, and your stay. You can adjust your new arrival time at the Florida destination because of that change. The schedule is a key component of the triple constraints used to manage and control the project.

Estimating cost and defining scope before you develop the schedule gives you the knowledge to build a schedule that meets cost expectations while delivering scope. In some cases the end delivery date is identified at the start of the project – the client or the sponsor has determined that on a specific date the project needs to be completed and you must build a schedule to comply. Additionally, other key dates or events that constrain the project along the way may be added to the project schedule. Remember, the project schedule is "an output of a schedule model that presents linked activities with planned dates, durations, milestones, and resources" (PMI 2017, p. 717). It's nothing more than a time prediction for the project, and it should be as complete as possible to be effective.

The benefits of a project schedule should be clear to anyone who has ever managed a business endeavor: if you don't know where you're going, then you could end up just about anywhere. A good project schedule:

- Is one of the foundational baseline tools. It provides the blueprint against which variation will be compared.

- Integrates project work into the most efficient and effective solution for the customer and the business.

- Helps to establish time agreements and expectations between the project team and key stakeholders. As the schedule is being developed, and at certain points in the life cycle of the project, the project team and key stakeholders will confirm, adjust, and reconfirm the key schedule dates and commitments.

- Helps the project team to manage the project. There is variation in everything. The project schedule guides the project team so that they know when action is necessary and when it's not. If you don't know which items in the schedule are critical and which aren't, you could make the wrong decision and make matters worse. This is the foundation of the monitoring and controlling system discussed in chapter 9.

◆ Helps the project team to determine if they can achieve the project objectives. If the schedule is complete, and all commitments are included, the schedule should enable the project team to know whether the project can achieve its time objectives.

◆ Enables effective communication of large amounts of data in a compact display format. "A picture is worth a thousand words" is one of the key reasons that you create a project schedule. In this chapter we'll discuss several different schedule views. Typically, project managers will select the view that conveys the information in a manner that most simply meets the needs of the audience.

Common Scheduling Problems

A schedule derived from poor planning data is at best a poor schedule. If the schedule is so critical to the effective management of the project, why are there so many ineffective schedule practices? Below are some of the common causes of ineffective schedules:

◆ **Not enough time dedicated to planning.** Historically, organizations just don't dedicate the proper time up front to plan the project schedule.

◆ **Lack of data.** Trying to plan the project schedule without key data such as resource availability, a complete or effective WBS, or consideration of risk seems foolish, but it's common.

◆ **Ineffective horizon.** Sometimes the project team tries to schedule too far in advance for a project they either don't fully understand or don't have enough information about. In this case it may be best to plan the schedule for smaller portions of the project instead of the whole project. For example, plan for just the requirements definition portion of the project, and once that's completed plan for the next phase, which may be design. When long-term elements of the project are not known or clear yet, or are contingent upon completion of earlier sections of the project, consider using the rolling wave approach discussed later in this chapter.

◆ **Not including the proper participants.** Dwight D. Eisenhower once said, "The plan is not as important as the process of planning." It's important that the planning session includes the people with knowledge of and responsibilities for the work in the plan. This builds their commitment, increases awareness of interdependencies between tasks and performers, and builds knowledge, which adds to project schedule effectiveness because the right people with the right knowledge are involved in the process from the start.

◆ **Poorly defined inter-relationships.** Sometimes a haphazard or poor approach is taken to identify the interdependencies between tasks. This hampers dynamic event analysis. In other words, we can't assess how a change in one part of the project will impact other connected parts of that same project.

Types of Schedules

To understand how schedules aid project effectiveness, it's helpful to discuss the key attributes of schedules and types of schedules. The best way to do that is to review some of the historical background of schedules.

Gantt Charts

In the early 20th century, work in factories was scheduled by quantity. This approach was effective when it was first used, but with competitive pressures of the early 1920s and the need to cut production times, a new focus was necessary. The mechanical engineer Henry Gantt thought that the focus on using quantity to determine schedules was misdirected and

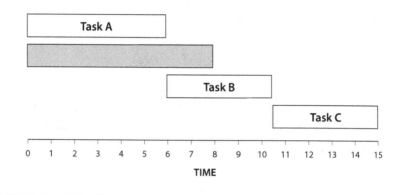

Exhibit 5-1. Simple Gantt Chart
In this example, the planned durations of three tasks (A, B, and C) are illustrated, with start times (left hand side of the bars) and finish times (right hand side of the bars). The gray bar denotes the actual duration of Task A (longer than planned).

that the focus should be on time. The solution that Gantt created was a bar chart that was used to both plan and control the work.

In the Gantt chart shown in Exhibit 5-1, the length of the bar indicates the length of time for the task. The plain white (or blank) bars indicate the planned start and finish for the task. The darkened bar below a task (in this case just for Task A) indicates actual performance. This type of schedule became very popular and widely used. It was even the main scheduling approach used in the planning and management processes of the Soviet Union. It's a simple, easy-to-understand tool. However, its simplicity made it a less effective tool as work became more complex, more interconnected. If you look at Exhibit 5-1, it's clear that the actual performance of Task A took much longer than planned. Because of that delay:

◆ What is the impact on Task B of this delay?

◆ Are both Tasks B and C pushed out to a later start date because of this delay in Task A?

Using this simple chart there's no way to know the answer to these two questions. As more and more sophisticated and complex projects were being undertaken, and the interconnectivity of the work was a critical issue,

87

other types of schedules became more popular, although improved Gantt charts are more widely used today.

Network Schedules

The network diagram is a type of schedule that's especially effective for displaying interconnectivity of the work. It consists of a graph that depicts the sequence in which project tasks are to be completed and shows the interdependencies of those tasks. The interdependencies are illustrated by the use of lined arrows between tasks. There are basically two general types of network diagrams: deterministic and probabilistic. In deterministic schedules each task has a planned duration, and the total duration of the project is a fixed value. In probabilistic schedules the durations of the tasks are random variables drawn from a probability distribution, and the total duration of the project is also a random number. Sometimes three-point estimates are used. Unfortunately, most schedules are probabilistic but are treated as though they're deterministic.

◆ **The arrow diagramming method (ADM)/program evaluation and review technique (PERT).** This method was created by the U.S. Navy, Booz Allen Hamilton, and Lockheed Corporation in 1958 in support of the Polaris missile and submarine projects. It's a scheduling technique that assumes that each activity finishes at a node from which others start. Exhibit 5-2 shows an ADM/PERT chart. In this example the circle numbered 1 is the start point for Task A. The node numbered 2 is the end point for Task A and the start point for Task C. The task name (in this case Task A) is written above the arrow (hence the name, arrow diagramming method) and the task duration is listed below the arrow. Normally the duration for the task is the result of using the three-point estimating technique (see chapter 4). The principle benefits of this type of diagram are the graphic depiction of the interdependencies and the probabilistic time frames that help to account for the uncertainly inherent in such an interconnected network.

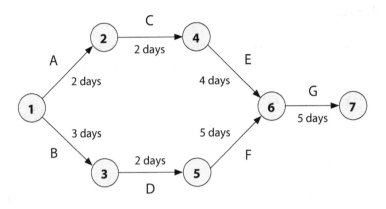

Exhibit 5-2. ADM/PERT Chart
The numbered circles represent starting points, the letters represent tasks, and the days represent the time it takes to accomplish the tasks (duration). You can easily see the interdependencies of the tasks in this diagram (Task C depends on Task A, Task E depends on Tasks A and C, etc.).

♦ **The precedence diagramming method (PDM)/critical path method (CPM).** These methods emerged from two sources: DuPont and IBM. DuPont is credited with creating the CPM method. Programmers from IBM are credited with creating the first precedence diagrams – they're easier to create than the arrow diagrams and they're normally based upon a single value for duration. The concept of critical path is applied in this scheduling method, which is important because it indicates which tasks cannot tolerate any delay. These tasks are deemed to be critical because any delay in them will delay the project if no corrective action is taken. We'll cover precedence diagramming in more detail later in this chapter when we talk about developing the schedule.

Additional Schedule Views

Project schedules can have additional specialized views. We've already talked about Gantt charts, arrow diagrams, and precedence diagrams. But the following views are used to convey project information more effectively to different audiences.

◆ **Milestone chart.** The milestone chart is a distilled view that shows just the milestones (significant points in time or key events). This view may be used on especially large projects that have a lot of lower-level management. On very large projects, particularly construction projects, there may even be a milestone manager assigned to just manage the accomplishment of that milestone.

◆ **Project summary view.** Most project software has the capability to roll up or summarize multiple subordinate tasks into an overarching summary task. On occasion it's helpful to roll up the tasks and display just the summary view of the project without the detail that may confuse some members of your audience.

Project Schedule Management Processes

Schedule management is time management. Every project has a time constraint and will require several discrete processes to effectively manage the accomplishment of project time. Those processes are:

◆ Plan schedule management

◆ Define activities

◆ Sequence activities

◆ Estimate activity durations

◆ Develop schedule

◆ Control schedule

These processes can be executed in the order listed or you may choose to follow a different flow. It's important, however, that all these processes are considered and undertaken as appropriate to avoid many of the challenges listed earlier in this chapter (see Exhibit 5-3).

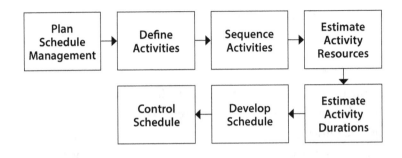

Exhibit 5-3. Schedule Management Process

Plan Schedule Management

This is the process of establishing the schedule management plan. First and foremost, the project team should decide on the level of formality (rigor) they will use to establish, monitor, and control the schedule. This will help them to select the policies, procedures, and documentation they will implement to ensure there are effective schedule management practices during the project. They should consider and, where appropriate, create a plan that specifies:

◆ Who will fulfill the various schedule roles

◆ What software will be used

◆ How the schedule will be communicated

◆ How the schedule will be stored

◆ How and by whom the schedule will be updated

◆ How and where the schedule will be displayed

◆ What information will be kept on each level of the schedule (level 1, 2, or 3)

◆ How the actual work progress should be communicated

Some typical project artifacts the team should review when building the schedule management plan include:

- Project charter/contract
- Project management plan
- Enterprise environmental factors
- Organizational process assets

In the process of developing your schedule management plan, it may also be helpful to engage the right subject matter expertise to ensure that the right activities are undertaken and the right rigor is applied. Additionally, consider reviewing similar prior project schedules and using organizational schedule templates where available, and analyze any other data (risk history, calendar impacts such as key shipping commitments, contract elements, downstream manufacturing availability, etc.) that may help to formulate the best schedule management plan.

Define Activities

This step is the process of identifying and documenting the specific activities and time elements that will be in the schedule to ensure that you produce the deliverables and achieve the project objectives. Normally some of this work will have been accomplished in an earlier define project scope process. The goal here is to ensure that all appropriate deliverables, activities, and tasks are identified and documented. Collectively these activities and tasks will form the work that is the foundation of the schedule. The tool most often used by project teams to identify project activities is the WBS (see chapter 3).

Sequence Activities

As discussed earlier in this chapter, one of the most important things to know about your project work is how activities are related to each other. In other words, what are the interrelationships between the activities that the project team needs to know to create the most effective project schedule flow? In the language of schedulers, a task that precedes a task is called a *predecessor.* Conversely, a task that follows another task is called a *successor.*

When defining activity sequence the person defining the relationships needs to consider whether tasks are mandatory or discretionary dependencies. Mandatory dependencies are tasks that must follow a defined order or sequence. For example, you must first write computer code before you can document it. A discretionary dependency is flexible and doesn't have to follow a defined path. It allows for flexibility in sequencing and performance. An example of a discretionary relationship occurs in home construction. Once the house is framed, you could do the electrical wiring next, or you could do the plumbing next, or you could do both.

Many project teams perform sequencing using simple tools such as yellow sticky notes or index cards. These tools enable the team to create the flow of events and create "what if" or alternative paths or flows. These simple tools are also popular because they can be placed on a table or a wall and arranged and rearranged by the team in a number of different ways to create the best possible schedule sequence.

Draw the Relationship Arrows

Once the flow of activities seems right, the team should next take the time to illustrate the relationship arrows between tasks. As stated earlier, relationships are illustrated using lined arrows between tasks. If you're doing this step manually, you can use tape, string, or lengths of sticky notes. This is especially helpful later in the process. When thinking about how activities relate to each other, remember that we're talking about dependencies. In an interrelated schedule, as one activity completes, the next activity can start. There are several ways in which tasks can relate to each other:

◆ **Finish-to-start (FS).** The most common type of relationship is the finish-to-start. The finish of the predecessor enables the start of the successor. Note: This is the default relationship in most project management software.

◆ **Start-to-start (SS).** In the start-to-start relationship you are binding two tasks together, defining one as the primary activity that will guide the subordinate activity. For example, if Task A is writing computer code and Task B is documenting that code, the arrow would come out of Task A (the primary task) and go to Task B (the subordinate task). This means that the start of Task B is aligned in some way with the start of Task A.

◆ **Finish-to-finish (FF).** In the finish-to-finish relationship (one of my friends used to refer to this as the "all Scandinavian" relationship), one of the tasks will function as the driving task, and the other (or others) will be linked as subordinate tasks. The goal of this approach is to have the finish of the subordinate aligned with the finish of the driver activity. Suppose, for example, that you have to cook a fine dinner that includes turkey and yams. The turkey normally takes four hours to cook and the yams just 20 minutes. The goal of the FF relationship is to start each task to ensure that they finish together. If all goes according to plan you'll have a nice meal. If you don't use this approach, you run the risk of having turkey with hockey pucks.

◆ **Start-to-finish (SF).** The start-to-finish relationship is the most abstract and difficult for learners to understand. In SF, the successor activity cannot finish until the predecessor activity has started. The best example of this approach occurred at a product development company. The company decided to establish a new production line and shut down the current line once the new line was up and ready. The completion of the successor (the new production line) enabled the ending and closure of the predecessor (the current line). Though not used often, this approach can be useful in the right circumstance.

Estimate Activity Durations

Once the team has assigned the resources, they can estimate the number of work periods required to complete the planned activities with those assigned resources. In this case we're talking about duration, which is the "total number of work periods required to complete an activity or work breakdown structure component" (PMI 2017, p. 705). Activity duration isn't always straightforward because it will be affected by many factors such as worker productivity, skill, or availability. Accounting for the fact that a less-skilled or less-available resource will increase the duration required to complete work helps us to create more realistic schedules, but until we know the resource by name this is hard to account for in the schedule.

Many project managers use an assumed average duration for this reason. Each activity should have a defined duration as a result of this process.

Develop Schedule

The develop schedule process puts all the preceding steps together. It combines the resource considerations, the activity considerations, and the timing/sequencing considerations to calculate an organized and dated roadmap for completing the project. It's the primary (and only) tool in the project domain that defines the dates for accomplishment and results. In calculating the schedule one common approach is the precedence diagramming method. This method uses both forward passes and backward passes to calculate a very informative type of schedule.

Exhibit 5-4 on the following page is an example of one form of PDM/ CPM diagram. Here the task names are in the boxes (nodes) and below each is the duration of the task. The numbers in the four corners of the box are the result of calculating the network, and they represent the early start date, the early finish date, the late finish date, and the late start date.

1. Calculate the Forward Pass

The first step in this process is to calculate the *forward pass*. From project start to finish, calculate the earliest that each activity can start and finish according to the logical sequence of work and the duration of each activity. In Exhibit 5-4 the forward pass begins in the upper left-hand corner of the first node (Task A). The upper left-hand corner is known as the early start (ES), the earliest planned start for this activity. Next calculate the upper right-hand corner of the node, called the early finish date (EF), the earliest planned finish of this task. The early finish is the result of adding the task duration to the ES minus 1 (for Task A the ES is 1 plus the duration of 3 equals 4, then minus 1 equals 3). The early start and finish dates are important because missing these target dates has an impact on the next tasks on the path in the network. Next you calculate the start of the successor tasks (those connected by the arrows). The ES of the successor is the EF of the predecessor plus 1. For example, if the early finish of Task A is 3, then the ES of Task B becomes 4 (3 plus 1).

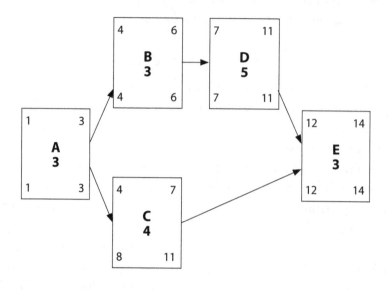

Exhibit 5-4. PDM/CPM Chart
In this example, task names (A, B, C . . .) are in boxes (nodes) with durations of the tasks listed under the names. The numbers in the corners represent the early start date (upper left), early finish date (upper right), late finish date (lower right), and late start date (lower left). You can see that this project is expected to be completed in 14 work periods.

Project schedulers should remember that when calculating the forward pass, and two or more predecessors feed into one successor, the highest EF of all the predecessors determines the ES for the successor. (The predecessor with the highest EF is commonly called the *driving predecessor* because it drives the calculation.) Continue until all tasks in the network have early start and finish dates calculated.

2. Calculate the Backward Pass

Once all the forward passes have been calculated, it's important to complete the network by calculating the *backward pass*. The backward pass identifies the dates that you cannot exceed to finish the project on schedule. If you miss these dates you'll add time to the project (if you don't take corrective action). So working backward from project finish to start, calculate the latest that each task must start and finish in order to meet the end date. The backward pass begins in the lower right-hand corner of the node, named the late finish (LF), the latest planned finish of this task. Next calculate the late start (LS), which is the lower left-hand corner of the node. The LS equals the LF minus duration plus 1.

In Exhibit 5-4, the LS for Task E is LF (14) minus duration (3) plus 1 equals LS (12). Next you calculate the LF of the predecessor tasks. The LF of the predecessor is the LS of the successor minus 1. So the LF for Task D is the LS for Task E (12) minus 1 equals LF (11). When calculating the backward pass, and two or more successors feed back into a single predecessor, the scheduler should take the lowest late start as the late finish of the predecessor. (The late start successor with the lowest LS is known as the driving successor because it's the one that drives the flow of the critical path backward pass calculation.) Referring again to Exhibit 5-4, when performing the backward pass, Tasks C and B feed back into Task A. The late start of Task B is 4 and the late start of Task C is 8. Therefore, you take the lower of the two (4), and that minus 1 becomes the late finish for Task A (3). Continue to calculate the LS and LF for all tasks until the network is complete.

There are many different methods for calculating the PDM/CPM network. This is just one of those approaches. It also is important to note that teams don't always need software programs to schedule. A team using rudimentary tools (yellow sticky notes or index cards) with written reports for monitoring and tracking can effectively schedule simpler projects. However, if the project becomes large, or is expected to grow into a large, more complex, or sensitive initiative, it's best to use project software to document, monitor, and control your project from the start.

3. Analyze the Schedule

The development of a good schedule is a time-consuming and challenging task. On particularly large projects, the team will be so happy to complete the effort that they may not perform critical evaluation steps. It's important to take the time to ensure that the schedule as planned accomplishes the key project objectives. This step should be performed *before* the schedule is shared with key stakeholders, and it should be performed by the project team. In this step the team is trying to analyze the results of their work in order to answer the following questions:

◆ **What is the total float (total slack) for each task?** Total float (TF) is the amount of delay planned in any one task in the network. The following formula can be used to calculate the total float of any task:

$$TF = LF - EF$$

Using Task C in Exhibit 5-4, total float equals LF (11) – EF (7) = 4. This task could be delayed up to 4 work periods (if all other factors remain constant) without delaying the end date of the project.

◆ **What is the critical path?** The critical path is the longest path in the network, and it's the shortest duration planned for the project. The critical path is identifiable as the path with the lowest float (normally 0 float or less). It's possible that there could be more than one critical path on the network. In some cases you may even want to force this approach (known as lean project management). When the project is scheduled with hard end dates, the scheduling logic will normally work backward from that end date. (Yes, it's possible to calculate the project schedule starting with the backward pass first.) In many cases, when the project is scheduled from a defined end date, the project team discovers that they're behind and should have started weeks ago.

◆ **What is the free float?** Free float is the delay that exists between an activity and its successor. The formula for calculating free float is:

Free float = ES of the successor – EF of the predecessor

Once again using Exhibit 5-4, the free float between Task E (ES 12) and Task C (EF 7) is 5. A good example of the use of free float involved a long-lead-time project to create a product that consisted of hardware, software, and packaging deliverables. The hardware was scheduled to be completed 12 February 2015, and the software (which would be loaded into that hardware) would be completed 15 January 2015. The packaging, however, which described all the features and functions of the software and hardware, was planned to be finished 2 June 2014. The free float between the packaging path and the other paths was approximately six months. This presented a problem to the project team because the features and functions in the final products (hardware and software) could change before the project was complete. This meant that all the packaging would have to be scrapped or re-worked at great cost. Free float is a helpful tool for managing interdependencies between tasks and paths on a project.

4. Validate the Schedule

To validate means to ensure that the schedule chosen is the best solution. To determine this you must ask some key questions:

◆ Can we meet the objectives established for the project (time, cost, and scope)?

◆ Is the overall schedule realistic?

◆ Is the work defined in the most effective, efficient manner?

◆ Is the work defined and ordered in a manner that's trackable?

◆ Where are the bottlenecks? What are those bottlenecks?

◆ Where is there risk in the schedule?

◆ Is the schedule realistic from a resource perspective (no resources over-allocated)?

◆ Is there executive management commitment to the dates on the schedule?

◆ Are key oversight activities included?

5. Adjust the Schedule

If the schedule has problems and requires adjustment, then the project team can use one or both of the following tools:

◆ **Lag time.** This is the addition of waiting time between tasks. A unique problem for project managers is the need to represent waiting time. For example, Task A is the writing of a contract, and Task B is the start of the work. Once the contract is written, then Task B will begin. But this could mean that you've started work without

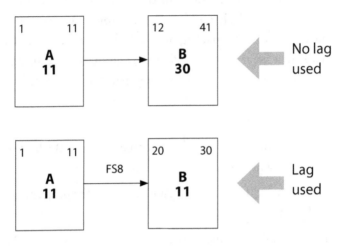

Exhibit 5-5. Lag Time

the proper contract in place if you haven't represented the delay that occurs when the contract travels through the mail, is reviewed by the customer, and is mailed back (a process of 8 days). You can accomplish this by using lag as shown in Exhibit 5-5.

◆ **Lead time.** This "is the amount of time whereby a successor activity can be advanced with respect to its predecessor activity" (PMI 2017, p. 709). Lead time can be effectively used to make up schedule time by compressing the plan. For example, the project is behind, so the project manager explores opportunities to accelerate the performance or start of some of the successor tasks. Lead time is not always an option, but when it is possible it can help the schedule get back on track. Lead is also known in some software as negative lag. Exhibit 5-6 demonstrates the concept of lead time.

6. Deploy the Schedule

Once the schedule has been adjusted and the project team agrees that it's effective and correct, it's helpful to deploy or send the schedule out into the organization to gain key stakeholder buy-in. You want to ensure that

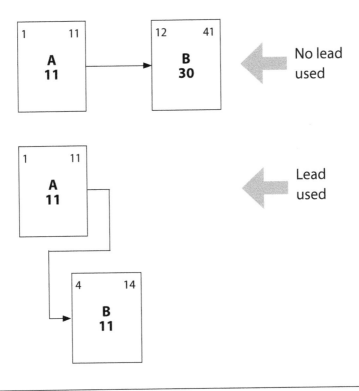

Exhibit 5-6. Lead Time

there's agreement on the start date, end date, and key milestones. This is a good time to highlight key points in the project where leadership involvement or key customer involvement is expected or required.

Control Schedule

Once the schedule is deployed it will require continual updating to remain effective for making project decisions. Schedule control is covered in detail in chapter 9.

TODAY'S PROJECT MANAGER has breakthrough scheduling concepts and tools available to assist in executing projects with excellence. Use them. There's no shortcut in creating an effective schedule.

CHAPTER SIX

The People Side of Project Management

I N 2010 CHRIS BOSH and LeBron James joined Dwayne Wade to form the "dream team" for the Miami Heat basketball team. Although all three had very successful NBA careers as individuals, they all considered themselves to be members of the team. Whenever the team won, no matter who was interviewed at the press conference, he always gave credit to the team, not to himself. If one of them made a mistake, the others patted him on the back and played harder to make up for him. They won as a team and lost as a team. Credit for the team mindset is given to motivator and team president Pat Riley. In 2013 this dazzling Miami Heat team set records when they won a phenomenal 27 games straight. The question is often asked, "What makes this team so great?"

This same question has haunted project managers for years. The answer lies in the successful leadership of a group of people. People are often the toughest part of a project to manage. Motivating team members who report to a functional manager can be extremely difficult. Whenever you have more than two people on a project there will be conflict, and that conflict must be managed. Communication both upward and downward can be time consuming and frustrating for the project manager, unless it's included as part of an overall communications plan.

103

Is a Team Necessary?

Let's first define a team. For our purposes, a team is a small number of people with complementary skills who are committed to a common purpose, agreed-upon performance goals, and an approach for which they hold themselves mutually accountable. This definition distinguishes a team from a mere group of people with a common assignment. We emphasize the definition because it's all too easy for potential teams to overlook the key aspects of it. In fact, it's really less of a definition than an essential discipline that, if applied, will produce efficient teams and optimal performance.

Although teams are standard in many organizations, it's important to realize that sometimes it's better to have one individual performing project tasks. Here are several instances where this might be true:

- **The task is routine.** If the project is routine (like building a new house – a simple construction project that's been done many times before) you probably don't need a team to accomplish most of the tasks.

- **Consensus is not important.** If one person has the needed expertise, experience, and knowledge – in other words, would be the primary subject matter expert on the project anyway – you may not need a team to perform the task.

- **Immediate action is required.** Going through the stages of team development can be time consuming. It will pay off in the long run, but if you have a short-term project that needs to be completed quickly, you may choose single individuals to perform the project tasks.

- **Compliance must be absolute.** The person doing the project task needs to have the support and authority to perform without having to justify every decision. Decisions must be final and compliance with the decisions is a must.

- **The whole is less than the sum of the parts.** This can happen when group pressure smothers individual creativity or when a group is dominated by one or two members and the rest just withdraw. Teams can be a waste of time and energy; they can enforce norms of low rather than high productivity. They can sometimes make notoriously bad decisions. Teams can exploit, stress, and frustrate if used when they're not necessary or when they're poorly designed and managed.

It may be advantageous to use a team under the following circumstances:

- Group acceptance is needed to implement a decision.

- Knowledge and skill from more than one person are needed to create the best product or decision.

- The group members possess specific information, problem-solving capabilities, and group process skills.

- There's time to meet as a group, discuss alternatives, and implement a decision.

- The highest quality or most effective solution is desired.

How Do You Build a Team from a Group?

Groups and teams are not the same thing. A group can be defined as "two or more individuals, interacting and interdependent, who have come together to achieve particular objectives." Exhibit 6-1 highlights the difference between groups and teams.

Work groups have a need or opportunity to engage in collective work that requires a joint effort. Therefore, their performance is merely a summation of individual efforts. There is little or no positive synergy that would make the overall level of performance greater than the individual effort.

A team generates positive synergy through a coordinated effort. Their individual efforts result in a level of performance that's greater than the sum of the individual outputs (Robbins 2005). During research for the book *The Wisdom of Teams,* Jon Katzenbach and Douglas Smith (1994)

GROUPS		TEAMS
Share information	**Goal**	Collective performance
Neutral (sometimes negative)	**Synergy**	Positive
Individual	**Accountability**	Individual and mutual
Random and varied	**Skills**	Complementary

Exhibit 6-1. Differences Between Groups and Teams

asked participants in their study, "What makes a group of people function as a team?" The top responses were:

- Common identity
- Common performance objectives
- Mutual accountability
- Complementary skills
- Shared purpose
- A shift from "me" to "we" mentality

In order to develop a common identity, ask yourself what benefits could accrue from being part of a team, for both individuals and the team as a whole, and use this information to help your team members to understand what's in it for them. Team members should agree to follow guidelines for working on your team. These are not objectives that will be used for evaluation purposes, but a mutual contract to ease the strain of working together under potentially stressful conditions.

Mutual accountability requires trust. Team members should have definitions of roles and responsibilities. The project manager should model honest, trustworthy behavior at all times in order to inspire like behavior from the other team members.

Shared purpose cannot be mandated from above; given good facilitation, the team will develop it as they participate and accumulate positive work experiences together. Successful teams agree on what's to be done for the project; individual team members understand their own as well as each other's role in achieving it.

When the group is fully functioning as a team, miracles can occur. When problems arise on the project, the team tries to resolve them as a team rather than searching for someone to blame. Blame is accepted as a team, and rewards are accepted as a team.

Managing Without Authority: The Art of Persuasion

Most of us want to influence others to consider and implement our ideas, but we don't have the formal authority to make things happen.

When you try to influence others over whom you have no formal authority, it's important to consider with whom you're dealing. Are you dealing with someone who wants the big picture, someone who wants everyone to be happy and get along, or someone who just wants the bottom line? These factors will influence your approach to a person, but the basics, as listed below, have to be addressed, whatever the personality or preferences of your audience:

- **Remember that communication is a two-way street.** Begin conversations with potential supporters with two goals in mind: to get information from them and to begin to share your ideas.

- **Use the pull concept.** Say briefly what your idea is and then ask for their thoughts about it. Encourage them to do the talking so that you can not only find out any objections but see gaps and flaws in your thinking. Listen carefully to find out who supports your ideas and who may have objections to them. As you start to gather new ideas, begin to shift your ideas to address the gaps and flaws. If your approaches to problems don't change over time as you gather viewpoints and information, you probably aren't listening well to others.

- **Talk to your potential objectors.** Talking with the people who may be against your ideas will be easier once you have some thoughts from potential supporters. Let others know that there are those who agree with you. "Yes, I understand your objection, and I had thought of that myself, but then Larry and Susan told me that..."

◆ **Establish credibility.** If you don't have the expertise, involve someone who does.

◆ **Look for common ground.** Always frame your proposals in a way that makes the common ground clear. "One thing that tech support and marketing share is the need to create satisfied customers."

◆ **Produce evidence to back up your assertions.** Examples, stories, experiences, metrics, and research help to make your position clear and validate your assumptions.

◆ **Connect emotionally.** Show your commitment to the position you are advocating and adjust your tone accordingly.

It's always more effective – and more ethical – to approach persuasion as the process of helping others to understand the benefits of your idea or approach rather than to view it as manipulation.

Five Stages of Team Development

Dr. Bruce Tuckman published his four-stage model of team development in 1965. He added a fifth stage, adjourning, in the 1970s. The theory is a helpful explanation of team development and behavior. It represents the stages that all teams go through, no matter the size or objective of the project. Tuckman's model explains that, as the team develops maturity and ability, relationships become established, and the team leader changes leadership style.

The team leader begins with a directing style, moves through coaching, then participating, finishing with delegating and an almost detached leadership style (see Exhibit 6.2 for a short discussion of leadership styles). At this point the team may produce a successor leader and the previous leader can move on to develop a new team.

The five stages of team development are as follows:

LEADERSHIP STYLES

Directive — Specific advice is given to the group and ground rules are established. The leader tells the team members what he or she wants and how it's to be done. No input is obtained from the team members.

Participative — Decision making is based on group consultation and information is shared with the group. The leader includes one or more employees in the decision-making process (determining what to do and how to do it). It's typically used when different team members have different bits of information. The leader maintains the final decision-making authority.

Coaching — The art and practice of inspiring, motivating, mentoring, and teaching team members. The leader guides the team members in the decision-making process, offering consulting and encouragement until a decision is reached. Final decision-making authority still rests with the leader.

Delegating — The leader trusts team members to make the decision, but ultimately the leader is still held responsible and accountable for the decisions that are made. Delegating is typically used when employees are willing and able to analyze the situation and determine what needs to be done.

Detached — The leader has complete trust in the decision-making capability of the team members. Typically detaching is used when the project is going well and requires little involvement of the leader. Team members and the leader are jointly responsible for the decisions.

Exhibit 6-2. Leadership Styles
Leadership style is the manner of providing direction, implementing plans, and motivating people. An important aspect of the team development process is the role the leader or leaders decide to play. Different styles of leadership may be appropriate for different teams or even for the same team at different stages in its development.

◆ **Forming.** In the forming stage, the project manager deals with each team member's need for belonging. This stage is about feeling comfortable in being part of the team. Team members need to know that they will be considered valuable.

◆ **Storming.** In the storming stage, the team deals with issues of power and control as individual team members try to establish their level of importance. This is when conflict is probably the most dangerous because team members tend to focus on their individual differences.

◆ **Norming.** The norming stage is when the team begins to focus more on task accomplishment and maintaining the psychological health of the team (as opposed to the individual). During this stage the team becomes more cohesive and open. There are still conflicts, but the conflicts are now focused on project issues rather than personal issues.

◆ **Performing.** When the team reaches the performing stage, it's working in the *we* rather than the *me* mentality. All individuals feel that they're team members, accept the team structure, and thrive in the team community. This is the most productive stage of the team, and good team leadership is aimed at minimizing the length of time it takes to get up to performing.

◆ **Adjourning.** Adjourning was added after the first four stages because it was felt that the team needed to have a sense of closure, especially if it had been in the performing stage for a long time.

One Project Manager's "Perfect Storm"

The storming stage is, without a doubt, the most difficult for the project manager to manage. This is where the project manager needs to use some creative management methods. If this isn't done, the team may never get out of the storming stage, and it will never be a fully functioning, productive team.

Several years ago I was asked to manage a project with high visibility and a short timeline, so it was extremely important that we hit the ground running. Some of the fifteen core team members were selected by me, while others were assigned because of their expertise in certain areas. During an elaborate kickoff meeting I noticed that one of the team members – I'll call him John – was speaking in low tones to each of the six core team members in attendance. They all had the same reaction to what he was saying. First they looked surprised, grimaced a bit, and then shook their heads. I had worked with John on several projects and had always been pleased with the results. He was very experienced and credible, and the team members looked to him as the informal leader of the team. It bothered me that he hadn't come to me with what he was telling the other team members, but within a day another team member informed me of what John had said.

Apparently, Joanne, one of the assigned team members whom I didn't know, was relatively new with the company and had worked on one project previously, one to which John had been assigned. He told the team members that Joanne had rarely attended team meetings, was always late on her assignments, and that he had concerns with regard to this project, considering her past performance.

Questions to Ask Yourself

As a project manager, how would you handle this storming situation? Play devil's advocate with yourself to find out what reaction your action would provoke from John, Joanne, and other team members.

Ask yourself, "Does it matter, and if so, why?" In this case there were two concerns:

1. Was it true? I was emphatic that team members attend meetings and get tasks done on time.

2. How would it affect the team? What would happen the first time Joanne came to a meeting late? The team might think that John was right and refuse to accept her as a team member.

Possible solutions:

◆   Talk to John – but John hadn't come to me. If I approached him he might well get defensive, deny it, or say that everyone had misunderstood him.

◆   Talk to Joanne – but I didn't know if what John said about her was true. She would have become defensive and wondered why I was picking on her.

◆   Talk to both of them together – but both would have been defensive.

◆   Talk to the previous project manager – but he had left the company and I had no idea where he had gone.

◆ Talk to some of the previous project team members – but soon the grapevine would have let Joanne know I was asking about her. Again she would have been defensive.

None of the above solutions addressed the two questions. I needed to get to the truth and address the team issues quickly. So I announced to the team that I was implementing a "Take a team member to lunch Wednesday" that would last two hours, would be informal in nature, and would be strictly a time to get to know each other. The first team member I invited to lunch was John. Because we knew each other fairly well, I told him I was pleased to have him on the team and would be interested in his assessment of the strengths of each team member. I purposely did not ask for the weaknesses because I didn't want to emphasize the negative aspects. He did so, and finally he told me what he had told the other team members. I did a little probing and found out that Joanne had missed about half the meetings, not most of them, and also that her tasks as a software tester had been toward the end of a very overdue project.

The next person I invited to lunch was Joanne. She was young, exuberant, and thrilled to be working on this project. She informed me that she wanted to become a project manager and looked forward to working with me on the project. I asked her what had been some difficulties on her previous project and she informed me that the project manager and her functional manager had hated each other. As a matter of fact, her functional manager had scheduled their mandatory, twice-monthly staff meetings at the same time that the weekly project team meetings were held. She was also very proud of herself that she had completed each of her tasks in about two-thirds of the assigned times since the project was so far behind. All of this answered my first question, "Is it true?" and even though it was true it didn't necessarily mean that it would happen on this project. My second challenge was to address the team members' attitudes toward Joanne. I asked her if she would like me to mentor her, which was received with great enthusiasm. With approval from her functional manager I assigned her some tasks that were to be completed by the next team meeting. I put her on the agenda first, thanked her in front of the team for her "above and beyond efforts," and laid to rest the team members' concerns.

The Bottom Line

Ask yourself what the specific concerns are and come up with possible solutions. Then ask what the outcomes could be. If the outcomes don't address your concerns, go back to the drawing board. Come up with a new solution that solves existing problems . . . instead of creating new ones.

Conflict Resolution Methods

Whenever two or more people are brought together, the stage is set for potential conflict. When conflict does occur, the results may be positive or negative, depending on how those involved choose to approach it.

Conflict becomes unhealthy when it's avoided or approached on a win/lose basis. Animosities will develop, communication will break down, trust and mutual support will deteriorate, and hostilities will result. When sides are chosen, productivity will diminish or stop. The damage is usually difficult or impossible to repair. Conflict is healthy when it causes the parties to explore new ideas, test their positions and beliefs, and stretch their imaginations.

It's important to recognize the reasons for conflict:

◆ Differences in needs, objectives, and values

◆ Differences in perception of motives, words, actions, and situations

◆ Unwillingness to:

• Work through issues

• Collaborate

• Compromise

◆ Differing expectations of outcomes

Some methods for dealing with conflict are:

◆ **Withdrawing (non-confrontational).** The withdrawing person ignores or passes over issues, or denies that issues are a problem. This method may be used if differences are too minor to matter, or too great to resolve. If resolution attempts might damage relationships or create even greater problems, withdraw from conflict.

◆ **Smoothing.** The smoothing person emphasizes commonalities and de-emphasizes differences. (For example: "I know we have our differences, but we both work for the same organization.") Use this method when it's not worth risking damage to relationships or general disharmony; of course, you must have commonalities for it to work.

◆ **Compromising.** Compromise requires the understanding that no one person or idea is perfect. There is more than one good way to do anything. When you're willing to give in order to get, compromise.

◆ **Forcing.** This dominating method might be summarized as: "I don't care how you feel or whether you agree, do it because I said so."

◆ **Problem solving.** This rational method confronts the problem, not the person. Problem solving examines several solutions and comes up with the one idea, or combination of several ideas, to best resolve the issue. Use a problem-solving style when parties can openly discuss issues without anyone having to make a major concession (Verma 1998).

◆ **Collaborating.** Collaboration involves incorporating several viewpoints to come to a consensus.

Managing Communication on the Project

Regardless of the environment, individuals on project teams must learn and practice effective communication skills. It's important to develop a communication plan that will meet the expectations of all the stakeholders. The project manager must identify the following components in order to develop an effective communication plan:

◆ **Audience.** Who is the audience for each communication? Check the project charter, project plan overview, and other project documents to determine audiences.

- **Message.** What message should go out to the audience? Examples include: What does the project need to communicate to its audiences? Who is authoring or sponsoring the message? How will it take place and in what steps or increments? What does the recipient need to do and by what date?

- **Intent.** Why is this communication taking place? What is the intended effect? What do we hope to achieve? What are the benefits?

- **Media.** How to communicate depends on the phase of the project, the audience, and other factors. It generally takes face-to-face communication to achieve buy-in, gain support, and motivate someone to action. At other times you can use hard copy print and electronic media, or combinations of media.

- **Timing and frequency.** Consider the scope statement, the evolving project plan, and the advice of project leaders and key stakeholders to determine a communication approach and timing. When do the various stakeholders need a report? How often should certain types of reports be generated?

- **Responsibilities.** For each message in the communication plan ask: Who will prepare the message, develop the media, and coordinate the delivery? Who will author or sign the communications? Who is the message from?

PROJECT MANAGERS OFTEN FOCUS too heavily on the technical aspects of a project and neglect the all-important human dimension. Yet the teamwork, communication, and stakeholder management aspects of a project manager's job are the areas where the greatest difference in outcomes can be achieved. Remember, in most cases project problems are people problems; conversely, people's successes translate into project success.

CHAPTER SEVEN

Managing Project Risk

RISK IS UNCERTAINTY that could affect a situation. There are two broad categories of risk: *pure risk* and *business risk*. Pure risk, which only has the potential for loss (such as a fire or a lightning strike), is most often dealt with by purchasing insurance or reducing exposure (through avoidance, for example). Business risk (also known as *speculative risk*), which has opportunities of gain or loss inherent in it, is where you can have a significant effect on the success of an enterprise.

There are two levels of risk that must be dealt with in a project (PMI 2017, p. 397):

- **Individual project risk** – "an uncertain event or condition that, if it occurs, has a positive or negative effect on one or more project objectives."

- **Overall project risk** – "the effect of uncertainty on the project as a whole, arising from all sources of uncertainty including individual risk . . ."

Traditionally many organizations have focused their efforts on identifying event-based risks, that is, risks tied to the occurrence or non-occurrence of an event. But emerging practices favor including non-event risks, where the project may experience *variability risk* (such as higher or lower productivity than anticipated), or *ambiguity risk* (such as uncertainty about how regulatory frameworks may develop).

In addition to the efforts to consider this wider scope of risks, organizations are emphasizing that risks be "owned" at the proper levels in the organization, and that a coordinated enterprise-wide approach is used to align risk management practices organization-wide. Tied to these efforts is the goal of making projects more resilient in order to deal with risks that are often not recognized until they occur (so-called *unknown-unknowns*). This trend has seen efforts to ensure adequate project budget and schedule contingencies to deal with such surprises, empowered project teams with processes that are flexible enough to deal with frequently changing projects, frequent reviews to detect early warning signs of emergent risks, and clear input from stakeholders regarding the adjustments to project scope and strategy (PMI 2017, 399).

Because it's misused by so many people as a synonym for risk, it's important to clarify one other term: issue. An issue is either a condition that exists (such as a risk that's already occurred) or a disagreement between stakeholders. Issues have a probability of one while risks have a probability of less than one. While a minor point, this precision in terminology will greatly assist the clarity of communications.

What is Risk Management?
And Why Do We Need It?

Risk management is something humans have engaged in since prehistory. Early humans balanced risk versus benefit in virtually every activity undertaken. The decision to kill an animal for food was balanced between the risk of injury and death to the hunter and the need for nutrition, hides, and bone for tools. Today that same balancing process continues. Now, as then, everyone does much of their risk management without being aware of it. People have some knowledge of what can hurt them and they avoid it, unless the expected reward for taking the risk is sufficient to outweigh the threat. People know things that they enjoy or that benefit them, and they undertake them or try to take advantage of those things as long as the counterbalancing risk is not too great.

The activity called *project risk management* extends throughout a project and actually starts before most project managers even become involved in the project. It usually begins when those who pick which projects will be pursued are first making their choices. The evaluation of positive and negative risks is normally a major input into their decision-making process. They will pick projects that, on balance, offer the best opportunities for positive results and the least chance of negative results. This reality demonstrates the objectives of project risk management. Those objectives are (PMI 2017, p. 395):

◆ To increase the probability and/or impact of positive risks (opportunities)

◆ To decrease the probability and/or impact of negative risks (threats)

While those objectives appear simple enough on the surface, the process of risk management can become complex because it occurs in the ever-changing environment where the project is being carried out. To make the initial judgments about which projects to pursue, decision makers must consider the intended results of the project, the team, corporate and external environments in which the project must be conducted, and the anticipated and unanticipated (yet possible) changes in those environments – all while evaluating the benefit-to-cost ratio of the project. Often the initial decision makers are operating with minimal or inadequate information. Often the project is little more than an idea, with vague and incomplete requirements, and the complexity of the project is unappreciated due to inadequate information and minimal analysis. This initial situation (with its uncertainty and incomplete information) makes the need for an *ongoing* risk management process even more critical. The failure to do proper risk management is one of the top five causes of troubled projects (PM Solutions 2011). So its importance is hard to overstate.

If all of the information about a project was known before we started it, and nothing would change, risk management could be done once and that would take care of all our concerns. However, as we all know, that isn't how the world works. Because you don't have all of the information you need at the beginning of the project, and because things change between the initial planning and the end of the project, the project risk management process must include some way of revisiting and updating the risk information, and appreciating the interplay between individual project risks and overall project risk. When risk management is done well, team members take proactive steps to protect the constraints, prevent surprises, prevent management by crisis, prevent problems from occurring or at least from escalating, and focus on doing things right the first time, thereby saving time and resources. To do this you must analyze each risk and break it down into its basic components.

The Components of Risk

Every risk has three components: *event, impact,* and *probability* (the backwards PIE). The event is simply what could occur (remember, this could be a positive occurrence or a negative one). The impact is the resulting change in the situation (such as a missed milestone or an early completion). Finally, there's probability (either objective or subjective) that must be gauged. We list the components in this order, like the word PIE spelled backwards, because that's normally the order in which they come to mind: What could happen, what would be the impact, and how likely is it to happen? Even if we don't know one or all of the elements of a particular risk, these components still exist.

Project Risk Management

If event, impact, and probability are present for every risk, known and unknown, how do you begin to identify them and deal with them? This is where project risk management comes into play. According to the *PM-BOK® Guide,* Project Risk Management is composed of seven processes:

◆ **Plan Risk Management** – the process of defining how to conduct risk management activities for a project

◆ **Identify Risks** – the process of identifying individual project risks as well as sources of overall project risk, and documenting their characteristics

- **Perform Qualitative Risk Analysis** – the process of prioritizing individual project risks for further analysis or action by assessing their probability of occurrence and impact as well as other characteristics

- **Perform Quantitative Risk Analysis** – the process of numerically analyzing the effect of identified individual project risks and other sources of uncertainty on overall project objectives

- **Plan Risk Responses** – the process of developing options, selecting strategies, and agreeing on actions to address overall project risk exposure, as well as to treat individual project risks

- **Implement Risk Responses** – the process of implementing agreed-upon risk response plans

- **Monitor Risks** – the process of implementation of agreed-upon risk response plans, tracking identified risks, identifying and analyzing new risks, and evaluating risk process effectiveness throughout the project

Each of these processes occurs at least once in a project, except for Perform Quantitative Risk Analysis, which may not occur if data are not available. The Project Risk Management processes must be revisited periodically, at least each time there's a known change in the project, whether it be a change in scope, time, resources, or any other conditions that could affect the project. Exhibit 7-1 demonstrates the process flow and iterative nature of project risk management. A brief description of each process follows.

Plan Risk Management

Plan Risk Management answers the question "How will the risks on this project be managed?" In this step, ensure that procedures are documented for how risks will be identified, assessed, prioritized, responded to, assigned status, and reported. Establish the frequency, formats, templates, and activities that will be used and the criteria that will be applied in classifying risks. With this level of detail you should be able to estimate the resources that will be required to comply with your risk management

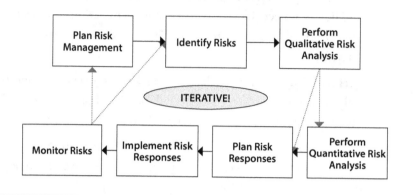

Exhibit 7-1. Risk Management Process

system. This process should also identify the risk attitudes of various organizations and individuals because they have a major impact on every aspect of risk management. Those risk attitudes can be broken into two aspects (PMI 2017, p. 407):

◆ **Risk appetite.** How willing is the person or organization to move forward in uncertain situations? Are they a risk taker or are they risk-averse? Ideally, these are expressed as measurable risk thresholds around each project objective.

◆ **Risk threshold.** How much uncertainty or impact will it require for the stakeholder to change from accepting the risk to not tolerating the risk? Project managers need to understand each stakeholder's risk thresholds for the various types of risk: schedule, cost, quality, customer satisfaction, impact to resources, and so forth, in order to devise and assess risk response options. Risk thresholds will be used in establishing definitions of probability and impact to be used when assessing and prioritizing individual project risks.

Project managers must consider what effects or disconnects may occur if a member of an organization has a very different risk attitude from that of their organization. The project team needs to consider how it will process and react to mixed signals, since failure to resolve such issues can result in reduced communications or disengagement by stakeholders who feel that their position isn't understood or appreciated.

An important part of this overall risk plan is the documentation system. Using a risk register or risk log is standard. Beginning as a primary output of the risk identification process, this record is further developed and utilized in each subsequent step of the risk management process. It typically includes the list of risks, the WBS numbers for the activities where the risk is present, a system for rating the significance of each risk, the planned response(s) to the risk, and any categorization of the risks. It may also include some analysis of the causes of each risk and/or a list of trigger conditions, which are tell-tale signs that the risk is about to happen. The documentation of trigger conditions is particularly valuable in helping the team to be on watch for the risks, giving all members notice of particular situations that require reactions (Exhibit 8-2 shows an example of a risk log). Other documents that relate to the risk management process include the issue log (which documents risks that have materialized and other matters that the team cannot agree upon) and the assumption log (used to record the unproven beliefs that have been considered true or certain for project planning purposes). The assumption log is also where project constraints (limiting factors that affect the execution of a project, program, portfolio, or process).

Identify Risks

The process of identifying risks should include the project team, subject matter experts (SMEs), stakeholders, and outside experts. It requires participants who are experienced and have a thorough understanding of project management techniques. Risk identification can be done using various techniques including brainstorming, SWOT (strengths, weaknesses, opportunities, and threats) analysis, and the nominal group technique. The nominal group technique is a silent style of brainstorming where ideas are submitted on slips of paper, posted on a wall, then grouped – by pairs of team members working without speaking – into logical groupings. Later the risks are prioritized by the team.

TOYOTA'S FIVE WHYS ROOT CAUSE ANALYSIS

Developed at Toyota, the Five Whys is an iterative question-asking technique used to explore the cause-and-effect relationships underlying a particular problem (or in our case, risk). The primary goal of the technique is to determine the root cause of the risk. Here's how it works:

- First identify the risk for which you want to determine the root cause

- Then ask "Why has this risk occurred?" and you'll come up with an answer.

- Next, take that answer and again ask "Why?" Now you'll get a second level answer.

- Repeat three more times. Usually, by the fifth iteration you'll have the root cause of the risk.

Exhibit 7-2. Toyota's Five Whys Root Cause Analysis

Teams often start with a list of risks from a prior project and then edit and amplify that list. One of the most important points to remember when identifying risks is to be very specific. "Resource availability" isn't specific enough. Without a list of specific risks you won't be able to plan specific risk responses. The required specificity can be achieved by stating risks using a cause-risk-effect format: specify the cause of the risk, what exactly the risk is, and what the effect will be on the project should the risk occur. The root cause can be determined using Toyota's Five Whys approach (see Exhibit 7-2). Using a root cause analysis approach to determine the cause reduces the likelihood of treating only symptoms. A cause and effect diagram is another tool that can be used here and in other applications of the risk management process.

Cause and Effect Diagrams

A cause and effect diagram (also known as an Ishikawa diagram, fishbone diagram, or, if it's really big, a Godzilla bone diagram) is a tool that helps the project team to have guided and detailed analysis of root causes of a given risk (see Exhibit 7-3). We use the term *guided* because the categories have headings such as people, method, material, machinery, or

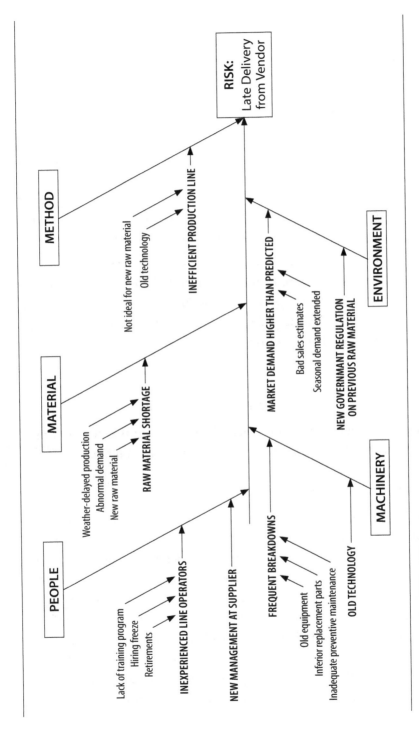

Exhibit 7-3. Cause and Effect Diagram

environment that guide the team in their search for possible causes. Once the root cause or causes are determined, the options for resolution are usually easy to identify.

The method for using this tool is as follows:

1. Define the risk, put it in the box at the far right of the diagram, and label it Risk.

2. Construct the categories for each bone of the diagram. Normally five bones is a minimum, and the headings used in Exhibit 7-3 are the general headings used when a team doesn't have categories of their own in mind. These generic categories cover the most common areas to be considered for any problem situation.

3. Brainstorm possible causes of the risk. The visual representation helps the team to focus, drill down, and identify items that may need further analysis because they're symptoms and not causes. In Exhibit 7-3 some of the primary causes have already been further analyzed, but you can continue that breakdown until you find the root causes.

Perform Risk Analysis

The main goal of performing risk analysis is to prioritize the list of risks. There are two types of risk analyses: *qualitative* and *quantitative*.

Qualitative Risk Analysis

Qualitative risk analysis is the process of assessing the impact and probability of the identified risks using subjective criteria. When conducting this type of analysis it's important to define the adjectives so that everyone has a similar frame of reference. This means that terms such as *high impact* need to be defined for this particular project. Some projects or stakeholders could tolerate large cost or schedule overruns before it would be considered high impact, while other projects or stakeholders might classify any overrun as a high impact. If you don't define the terms used, the results can vary greatly based on the raters' experiences and personal risk appetites. However, the desire for more uniform subjective

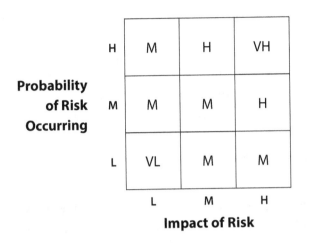

Exhibit 7-4. Nine-Block Matrix
Use this risk analysis tool to determine the risk event value (low, medium, or high) by comparing the probability of the risk occurring and the impact of the risk. A risk with a high probability of occurring and a low impact will have a medium risk event value. The tool helps the project team separate vital risks from the many trivial risks.

criteria must not nullify legitimate risk thresholds of various stakeholders.

There are many tools used by project teams to assess risk event value (also known as risk severity or risk exposure). When using qualitative data, the project team can use the nine-block matrix. This matrix is typically developed at the organization level and applied by the project manager and the project team when assessing and prioritizing risks. The benefit of this tool is that it allows a large number of risks to be sorted by the project team relatively quickly. This process helps the team to differentiate the vital risks from the many trivial ones. It's a simple tool to use – the vertical axis in Exhibit 7-4 consists of the range of qualitative probabilities of the risk (high, medium, and low) and the horizontal axis consists of the same values for assessed risk impact. The process for using this tool is as follows:

1. Define each probability and each impact criterion. These values will often be project specific. For example, high probability ranges from 99 percent down to what number? Then set the boundaries

for the other probability levels. Next, determine what a high impact is. Many project teams will define it in relation to the project constraints: cost overrun, schedule overrun, incomplete scope, and quality. These items must be defined before you can do qualitative analysis. The single nine-block matrix set up with impact values for negative risks (threats) is not really compatible with analyzing positive risks (opportunities) – a separate matrix with its own probability and impact criteria definitions is required.

2. Assess each risk for its probabilities.

3. Assess each risk for its impact.

4. Using the results of steps one and two, find the intersection of the probability rating and the impact rating to discover the assessed risk event value or severity.

5. Repeat this procedure until all risk events have a risk event value.

6. Sort the risks into groups of common values (high, medium, and low).

Quick exercise: Using Exhibit 7-4, determine the risk event value for a risk with a medium probability and a high impact. Answer: It's a high-value risk. Note: The nine-block matrix used in this material is not scientific. Each organization should determine its own values for each quadrant in the matrix.

Quite often, when the team has sorted the risks using the nine-block matrix, they'll have groups of risks (very high risks, high risks, medium risks, low risks, and very low risks). Organizations can't afford to spend money mitigating each risk, so they need to continue the prioritization process by working to understand the interrelationships between risks. It's quite often the case that one key risk, if dealt with appropriately, will have a beneficial domino effect on the other high risks in the group. This process helps the team to understand which risks are most worthy of attention. One of the key tools used to help in this process is the pairwise comparison matrix (see Exhibit 7-5). This tool helps the project team to rank risks with the same risk event value against each other. The process for using this tool is as follows:

	A	B	C	D	E	Total	Rank
A		B	A	A	A	3	2
B			B	B	B	4	1
C				C	C	2	3
D					D	1	4
E						0	5

Exhibit 7-5. Pairwise Comparison Matrix
This tool helps the project team to rank risks in a common group against each other. Risk A (left column) is dominant over risks C, D, and E (across the top), totalling 3 in the right column. Risk B is dominant in 4 comparisons and is, therefore, the most influential in this group of risks.

1. Each of the risks in a group (very high risk group, high risk group, medium risk group, low risk group, or very low risk group) is assigned a letter.

2. Create a matrix similar to Exhibit 7-5 and post it in clear view of all team members.

3. Using a disciplined approach, a facilitator guides the team in comparing Risk A against each one of the other risks. The comparison is done using a common question applied to each pairing. For example, "Which risk has a greater impact?" The team records the dominant risk in each box.

4. The process continues, comparing all risks against each other.

5. Next, record the number of occasions that each risk is dominant in the entire matrix in the Total column. Using Exhibit 7-5 as an example, Risk B is evaluated as dominant the most, 4 times, so record the number 4 in the Total column.

6. Finally, analyze the results. The risk with the highest number in the Total column is most influential, most dominant. Enter a 1 in the Rank column for this most dominant risk. The risk with the second highest total is the second most dominant and will receive a 2 in the Rank column, and so forth. Ties are resolved by noting which of the risks was dominant when those risks were compared to each other.

Through this process the team is able to establish a priority for the risks in that grouping and as a result can determine effective investment and mitigation strategies for dealing with each risk.

Qualitative risk analysis is the most commonly applied approach, and sometimes the results of this analysis are expressed in numbers. But you must be careful not to confuse those results with the outcomes of quantitative risk analysis.

Quantitative Risk Analysis

Quantitative risk analysis is another method for analyzing risk that uses a numerical analysis. Many organizations and projects don't have enough hard data to use this level of analysis. Ideally, quantitative risk analysis follows qualitative risk analysis, and the purpose of this activity is to quantify risk resolution mitigation options. This enables the project team to select the best risk management option with the most effective return on investment.

Quantitative risk analysis typically starts with the collection of data. The data are displayed by the use of various tools that enable effective analysis. The tools range from simple rough-order-of-magnitude (ROM) assessments to more-detailed computer simulations. Some of the more common tools used for risk quantification include:

◆ Sensitivity analysis
◆ Expected monetary value (EMV)

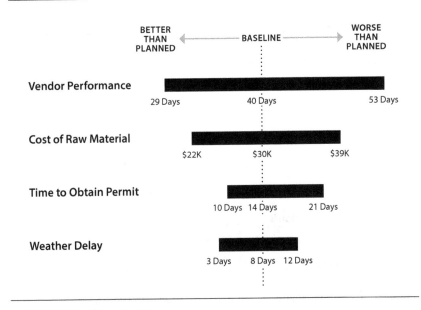

Exhibit 7-6. The Tornado Diagram
This diagram represents which risks can have the greatest effect on the project.

◆ Decision trees (a common application of EMV)

◆ Project simulations

Sensitivity Analysis. Sensitivity analysis assists in identifying which risks have the greatest potential impact on the project. It can be used to answer the "What if?" questions. One sensitivity analysis tool is the tornado diagram, which displays the comparison between risks with a wide range of possible outcomes and risks with a narrower range of possible outcomes. It's a bar chart where the categories are displayed vertically instead of in the usual horizontal presentation, and the values are displayed in bars around a central axis (which represents the baseline value for that risk) in a range with negative impacts on one side of the baseline and positive impacts on the other (see Exhibit 7-6).

The tornado diagram shows which risks can have the greatest effect on the project. The dotted line represents the baseline (the most likely estimate); to the left of the dotted line is the optimistic range, to the

Expected Monetary Value of Option A is $4,700 ($6,000 – $800 – $500)

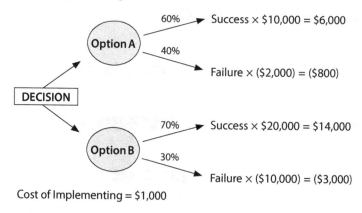

Cost of Implementing = $500

Option A

60% → Success × $10,000 = $6,000

40% → Failure × ($2,000) = ($800)

DECISION

Option B

70% → Success × $20,000 = $14,000

30% → Failure × ($10,000) = ($3,000)

Cost of Implementing = $1,000

Expected Monetary Value of Option B is $10,000 ($14,000 – $3,000 – $1,000)

Exhibit 7-7. Decision Tree

right the pessimistic range. Analyzing the comparative potential helps the team to focus on opportunities to pursue and which threats require a response.

Expected Monetary Value. Expected monetary value uses the probability and value of each possible occurrence to provide an understanding of the possible alternative outcomes in a situation. The calculation is achieved by multiplying the probability of each occurrence by the monetary gain or loss that will result from that choice. The results can be represented in a variety of ways, but a decision tree is one of the most popular.

Decision Trees. Decision trees are used to understand the potential outcomes in a circumstance where several options exist. In Exhibit 7-7 there are two options under consideration for this risk. Option A has a 60% probability of success and a 40% probability of failure. The benefit for accomplishing a successful Option A is $10,000. The cost to you if this option fails will be $2,000. The expected monetary value of Option A is equal to Success ($10,000 × .60 = $6,000) minus the cost of Failure ($2,000 × .40 = $800) minus the cost of Implementing the option ($500). That equals $4,700 ($6,000 − $800 − $500) as the overall value (or expected monetary value) for Option A. The second consideration is Option B. Success for Option B, using the same estimating approach as above, results in $14,000. The cost of Failure is $3,000. The cost of Implementing the option is $1,000. Therefore the overall expected monetary value of Option B is $10,000 ($14,000 − $3,000 − $1,000). When the project team compares the two options against each other, they will use this data to determine which option is the best course of action in response to the risk (Option B in this example).

Tools like this provide important information to consider when making a decision, but you should take other factors into account as well, such as business context and stakeholder needs. While Option B offers more than twice the expected monetary value of Option A, some organizations couldn't afford the risk of taking Option B − if it were to fail, the total negative impact of $11,000 (the cost of implementing the option plus the cost of failure) might be more than the organization could stand.

Project Simulations. A major challenge for the project environment is the fact that much of what happens is dynamic complexity. In dynamically complex situations cause and effect are subtle, and the effects of the actions you take to influence the situation aren't immediately obvious and may not be for some time. This complicates the risk management process because we need to know now what the best, most cost-effective actions are.

Computer simulations are very helpful with dynamically complex situations. Typically a computer model is created, and then the outcomes are calculated using various input values spanning the range of possibilities. These simulations aid in understanding the range and possibilities of outcomes and are another approach often used to answer "What If" questions. Approaches using computer-aided design (CAD), prototyping tools, Monte Carlo analysis, and commercial tools such as Crystal Ball and @Risk are helpful in mastering particularly complex risk scenarios. In most cases organizations have specialists in the use of these tools to call on to help your project team.

Plan Risk Responses

Once the prioritized list of risks has been developed using the risk analysis processes, decisions must be made on how to handle each risk (with the team agreeing on the plan). This process is called Plan Risk Responses. The strategies to deal with risks can be broken into four groups: strategies for threats, strategies for opportunities, contingent response strategies, and strategies for overall project risk (PMI 2017, pp. 442–46).

Strategies for Negative Risks or Threats

- ◆ **Escalate.** This approach is used when the project team or the project sponsor agrees that a threat is outside the scope of the project or that a proposed response would exceed the project manager's authority. Escalated risks are managed above the project level (e.g. – program level, portfolio level, or other appropriate part of the organization), so the project manager needs to determine the right person or group to notify, and then communicate the details to them. But merely communicating it to them is not enough – the project manager must verify that the risk is accepted by the relevant person or group. Once the escalation is accepted, the team so annotates their risk register and can discontinue monitoring the risk. As a practical matter, the team will need to determine if the threat still poses any further danger to the project in case it wasn't eliminated by the action party.

- ◆ **Avoid.** In this approach the project management plan is changed to eliminate the risk. This may involve not doing part of the job or changing the process so that the risk is no longer present. Contractors use this approach when they decide to not bid in response to a request for bid or a request for proposal.

◆ **Transfer.** In this approach the problem is shifted to another party such as a contractor or an insurance company. The goal of this approach is to share or transfer in whole or in part the management or the impact of the risk. While increasing the cost to reduce the risk, hiring a specialist to do the work may also have additional positive impacts such as increasing the quality and/or speed of completion of the work. Contract clauses are the most common way to transfer risks. Note that transfer can be abused by organizations when they knowingly shift hidden risks to contractors without providing full disclosure. Performance bonds, warranties, and guarantees are additional examples of this strategy

◆ **Mitigate.** This involves taking action to reduce the probability of the risk's occurrence or limit its impact. Many organizations take actions to foster both results. This is demonstrated by the safety approach taken in many manufacturing plants where workers receive training about accident prevention (reducing the probability of accidents) and are required to wear personal protective equipment, such as safety glasses, gloves, steel-toed shoes, and hearing protection (reducing the impact or severity of accidents).

◆ **Accept.** This approach is generally used when the cost to avoid, mitigate, or transfer is believed to be more than the cost of the problem should it occur. Accept can be passive (which means the team will have to deal with the risk when it occurs) or active (which includes actions such as creating a contingency reserve of money, time, and/or resources). Both of these accept approaches are in common use.

Strategies for Positive Risks

◆ **Escalate.** When the project team or the project sponsor think that the opportunity is outside the scope of the project, or where the proposed response would exceed the project manager's authority, this strategy is appropriate. The project manager must determine the appropriate individual or group to be notified and communicate the pertinent information to them. Just as with escalation of negative risks, it's important that ownership of the opportunity is accepted by the appropriate individual or group. While the team should annotate the risk register regarding the escalation, they can discontinue monitoring of the opportunity.

◆ **Exploit.** Pursue the positive risk so that it's no longer just an opportunity but something that's made an active goal of the project. An exploit strategy usually involves taking actions to increase the certainty that the event has a positive outcome.

◆ **Enhance.** In this approach you increase the probability and/or the impact of the opportunity in a strategy that's the opposite of the mitigation strategy used for negative risks. This is accomplished by promoting conditions that will cause the opportunity to happen or by creating conditions that make the targeted risk more valuable to the project. This situation could arise where training is required for some of your team members, and you extend the positive impact by including more team members or other employees in the training, thus getting more bang for your buck. Good managers use this approach in many business situations, such as identifying projects in need of funding and preparing all of the necessary paperwork so that any surplus monies can be diverted to the ready and waiting opportunities.

◆ **Share.** Sharing is the action of bringing in a third party to help pursue an opportunity. This can be done by partnering with organizations or individuals who are better able than the original project organization to make this part of the project happen. An example of this technique would be to partner with another company that has an existing proven software application and successful integration experience to meet a project need, instead of developing that capability in-house or turning down the opportunity. Another sharing approach would be to license the product to another company for manufacture and distribution when that's more cost-effective than making it in-house.

◆ **Accept.** When used regarding an opportunity, to accept means to be willing to take advantage of an opportunity when it occurs, but not to actively pursue it.

Contingent Response Strategies

Often called contingency plans, these are used only when triggered by certain events. The project team will develop response plans for some of the risks, but they'll take no further action until the triggering condition occurs. These often include budget or schedule contingencies that are only used under certain conditions. Some common examples of contingent response plans include an organization's business continuity plan or emergency plan.

Strategies for Overall Project Risk

These strategies deal with the combined effects of individual project risks and other uncertainty. While the risk response strategies are the same as those for individual risks, the project team must consider how the net results of balancing threats and opportunities compares to the project's risk tolerance.

◆ **Avoid.** This approach may be used when the overall project risk is negative and is beyond the agreed-upon threshold. Changing the project by removal of high-risk elements in the scope is one of the ways this may be accomplished. If such actions fail, the most extreme form of this strategy would be to cancel the project.

◆ **Exploit.** This strategy would be appropriate where the overall project risk is positive and exceeds the agreed-upon positive threshold. This involves taking actions to adjust the positive risk threshold or to improve the overall project opportunity. Examples include adding elements to the project that add value to stakeholders.

◆ **Transfer/share.** Where the overall project risk is negative and high, a transfer strategy can help reduce it. Similarly, where the overall project risk is positive and high, a share strategy is appropriate. Several common business approaches could solve either situation, such as sharing risk between vendor and customer (via contract type and/or special contract clauses), subcontracting parts of the project, or setting up a joint venture or special-purpose company.

- ◆ **Mitigate/enhance.** This strategy is used to improve the overall project risk. Just as with individual risks, the mitigate approach would be used if overall risk is negative, and enhance would apply if overall risk is positive but the project team wants to improve it. The following actions could apply for either situation, depending on how they're used: replanning the project; changing scope, schedule, or budget; or changing resource allocations.

- ◆ **Accept.** The organization may pick this option where no strategy is found to affect the overall project risk. An active acceptance approach could include creating overall contingency for the project. Should the organization choose this strategy, it's imperative to continue to monitor overall project risk to ensure that this strategy is still appropriate.

Implement Risk Responses

After the project team agrees on how to address overall project risk and specific project risks, implementing risk responses ensures that the agreed-upon actions are carried out as planned. The implementation of risk responses has been a weak point in many projects. Frequently project teams have done a good job of risk identification, analysis, and prioritization, and of selecting appropriate risk responses, but for various reasons the planned responses weren't carried out. Causes of those failures to properly implement risk responses have included a lack of clear roles and responsibilities definitions, overallocated resources, individuals or groups responsible for implementing the response being tasked with higher priority work, and inadequate oversight and management by the project manager or project sponsor. The *PMBOK® Guide* makes clear what is needed (PMI 2017, p. 450):

> Only if risk owners give the required level of effort to implementing the agreed-upon responses will the overall risk exposure of the project and individual threats and opportunities be managed proactively.

Project teams must ensure that they actively implement a policy to regularly review the status of risk responses and those charged with carrying them out.

Monitor Risks

The final step in Project Risk Management, Monitor Risks, is a broadranging activity that involves tracking the progress and effectiveness of the risk plan and dealing with changes to the plan (including new risks and situations that make the then-existing plan less than optimal). This activity is ongoing, beginning with the completion of the initial risk plan, and involves all of the risk management steps as the project team periodically and regularly monitors project performance, audits, reassesses existing approaches to the work and to problems that develop, does variance and trend analysis, and determines if project reserves are adequate.

As part of Monitor Risks, the project team must:

- Monitor implementation of agreed-upon risk response plans
- Track identified risks
- Watch for new or redeveloping significant risks
- Analyze change requests for their risk potential or effects on the existing risk plan
- Monitor for project environmental changes that could require reaction, prevention, or avoidance planning
- Monitor for and prevent unintended results of project or risk response actions
- Evaluate risk process effectiveness

Making It Real

There are some common tools and approaches that assist in making this part of the process more effective.

First, every identified risk should be assigned to a team member. That person will be responsible for monitoring that risk for the team, keeping the risk log updated, and advising the team of any significant change in the risk.

Second, it's essential that risk be a major topic of discussion in status meetings. Remember: What gets reported on gets done! So make risk the third item on your status meeting agenda. After reviewing what's happened on the project and then discussing upcoming events, as long as risk is in the top three items and gets covered, all should be well. As part of this approach the project manager should have those individuals assigned to specific risks report on them to the team. Normally only the top five or ten risks are reported on each week, unless there's a particular question about a given risk or a significant increase in the risk's overall rating.

This regular reporting procedure helps to keep team members focused on monitoring the risks for which they're responsible and keeps the issue of risk higher in the team members' priorities. By keeping team members informed of the risks and enhancing their awareness of the risk management plan, the project manager also increases the chances of risks and trigger conditions being recognized earlier. Early recognition often provides the team with opportunities to avoid or effectively minimize the impacts of the risk. Done correctly, this creates the overall condition of risk awareness in the organization and greatly improves overall risk management.

Third, communication is essential to this process. Everybody who needs to know, needs to know! You must have a system for disseminating project information (including risk management information) that's clear, concise, complete – and used! Today most team members suffer from information overload. They need to receive effectively crafted information – information that they need, in a form that's most helpful to them, that can be quickly reviewed and acted on, and that can be accessed in the future with a minimum of effort.

Fourth, one tool that can assist in this process (and which is applicable to many project status communications) is a reporting template and standard operating procedure. By establishing this procedure at the beginning of the project (such as at the kickoff meeting), the project manager can bring some needed order and uniformity to the process while requiring concise communications.

The template can be used for reporting any project status item, including risk, and it promotes the quick dissemination of information to those who need it. The template, if properly designed, can also serve as the basis for the lessons-learned database, overcoming a frequent challenge experienced by project managers trying to gather lessons learned at the end of a phase or project. The template, after its subject line and standard routing, should include five questions that are applicable to virtually all projects:

- What happened?
- What did the project plan say to do about it?
- What was actually done?
- How did the action taken work?
- What are the recommendations for next time?

These questions provide the basis for informing those who need to know; but in order to keep this system manageable it's appropriate to limit the responses to each question to about two short sentences. For such a system to work, the information must be transmitted quickly after the event to the project manager (usually within twenty-four hours), and the project manager must ensure that anyone who has a need to know gets a copy of the message. These messages, after being acted upon, should then be archived so that they're available for the team to review in the lessons-learned activities at phase or project end. As with all project management activities, rapid and accurate reporting must be appreciated – even rewarded. If the project manager shoots the messenger, he or she will soon run out of messengers!

In summary, here is a risk management reality checklist:

- Reality Check #1: Risk management is an ongoing activity.
- Reality Check #2: Not doing good risk management is one of the top causes of troubled projects.

- Reality Check #3: Risk management is one of the areas that's usually shortchanged early in the project, either by not being done completely or by managers who reject some of the risk analysis or risk responses.

- Reality Check #4: Risk management can be implemented at any time in a project. If you didn't start doing it at the beginning of the project, don't despair!

- Reality Check #5: When done correctly, risk management provides a high return on investment.

IT'S UP TO THE PROJECT MANAGER to ensure that good risk management practices are adhered to and that the results of risk management are documented. Document your recommendations, even if they're ultimately not approved, because that information will assist in your post-project review and in developing lessons learned for future projects.

CHAPTER EIGHT

Executing the Project

Where the Rubber Meets the Road

I N AN EARLIER CHAPTER we compared a project to a road trip, and we'll continue to follow that analogy. The trip plan has been done, and the team is getting ready to depart, but before every trip begins, a final check is needed to prevent false starts.

Getting Traction

Now begins the actual work on the deliverables of the project. The execution phase of the project is about managing and controlling outcomes. Managing and controlling activities are based on all of the work done in the planning phase. Anyone who has taken a trip planned by someone who didn't come along on that trip can probably relate to the situation where instructions or plans weren't completely clear or logical. Some projects have this characteristic because, sadly, for some project managers and teams the execution phase is the first time that they've had any contact with the project. To their detriment, some organizations don't get project managers involved until the beginning of project execution, so those project managers and their teams have had no input in the planning, estimates, or schedules. As a result team buy-in is usually low, and the project plan (if any) hasn't benefited from the diverse experience of the team members and may not even reflect the reality that they encounter at the beginning of the execution phase. Projects that start out this way often set the team up for failure, or at least for unreasonable time schedules and inadequate budgets. A high percentage of troubled or failed projects have taken this ill-advised path. To reduce the chances of problems, project teams should do some of the project initiation processes and teambuilding exercises that were described in chapters 2 and 6.

Checking the Roadmap

Ideally, your project begins with the project manager and the project team (if assigned) involved in planning the work and developing the schedule and estimates. Then, at the start of the execution phase, they shift their primary emphasis from *planning the work* to *working the plan* that they've developed. The first thing to be done is to identify the project manager and team members (or the team leads and members for subparts of the project, if it's organized that way). Once the team is in place they should review the state of the project by first reviewing the project documents that already exist. Remember that some of the major causes of troubled projects are (PM Solutions Research 2011):

- ◆ Insufficient involvement by customer or sponsor
- ◆ Lack of a qualified project manager
- ◆ Failure to follow a project management methodology
- ◆ Poorly defined/incomplete requirements
- ◆ Not establishing/not following a change management process
- ◆ Not establishing/not following a risk management process

This means that the team that institutes and adheres to processes that eliminate or minimize the occurrence of these typical causes of trouble should have a much higher success rate. That being said, items that should be reviewed include everything developed in the initiating and planning processes to date, from the project charter and scope statement to the schedule and the resource lists.

Trip Plan Complete? Documentation Review

The documentation review determines what documents you have and how complete they are. Next, all your documents need to be updated. Just as in our theoretical road trip, if there have been changes, or new or additional information has become available since the trip was initially planned, then the trip plan must be updated. How much information is enough? What level of detail is needed? It depends.

Because the amount of project management activity should be appropriate for the complexity and needs of the project, there's no clear formula for exactly what's required. Scalability is the controlling principle. For a short trip you might only need a street name or a landmark to note a critical turn, while a long or complex route might require multiple maps, lengthy instructions, and various alternate routes in case of delays, detours, or traffic backups. The key to successful project management is to have enough documentation and tools to successfully manage the project without wasting any effort on excessive activities or documentation (see Exhibit 8-1).

Verifying Location and Route Conditions

In trip planning you might contact an auto club or state highway department for information or validation of the trip plan. Similarly, if a project manager or team is taking over a project that's already underway, it may be wise to request a peer review (where another project manager documents the state of the project) or a project audit (where some outside group evaluates the present state of the project and the quality of its documentation). These types of reviews can be used to re-baseline the project so that the new project manager and/or team can eventually receive credit or blame for what they've done and not for what they've inherited. It's appropriate to meet with key stakeholders as part of this review.

Once the review is complete and necessary updating is done to existing documents and processes, the team may find that various documents and processes are missing from the inventory. It's then appropriate for the project manager and team to complete the missing activities. The results

DOCUMENTATION REVIEW

- Project charter or other initiation document (e.g., customer contract)
- Business case
- Kickoff meeting documentation
- Completed checklists and documentation from initiating processes
- Organizational process assets (info, data, processes — typical example in corporate setting is vendor management/procurement management process)

Project Plan

- Stakeholder list (part of stakeholder management plan, if it exists)
- Business requirements document & traceability matrix
- Customer acceptance criteria
- Scope statement (produced by project team and more detailed than one in project charter)
- Work breakdown structure
- Project schedule
- Project budget
- Staffing plan
- Risk management plan
- Assumptions log
- Communication plan (probably also part of stakeholder management plan, if it exists)
- Change control plan

Execution and Control

- Status reports
- Scope change requests
- Customer satisfaction surveys

Closing

- Lessons-learned documentation
- Project closeout report

Meetings

- Agendas
- Minutes
- Issue/action item log
- Presentations

Exhibit 8-1. List of Items to Review in a Documentation Review
The number of items in the list depends on when the project manager is doing the review — if the review occurs later in the project life cycle then more documentation should be available and complete.

of the document reviews, updates, and process completion may raise the need to again consult with the project sponsors from the project manager's organization and the client organization to advise them of the status of the project and to recommend changes in the schedule and/or the budget.

Some teams have tried to leave some of these items to be completed as they're needed (known as a just-in-time strategy); however, waiting to complete these processes is usually going to be more expensive and time-consuming in the long run. It's a matter of "pay me now or pay me later," and paying later (to fix problems) can often cost ten to a hundred times as much as fixing something early in the project planning or execution phases.

Once all of the planning is completed, it's appropriate to update the stakeholders on any changes since the last meeting with them. This updating may be part of an execution phase kickoff meeting.

Critical Questions

At the completion of the documentation review and updating processes the project manager and team should have very clear answers to questions such as:

- What are the customer acceptance criteria?

- What metrics will be used to track the project status?

- What are the details of the project management information system, including the project repository and/or shared drive, for documenting project information?

- What are the roles and responsibilities of each team member?

- How will communications (internal and external) be handled and by whom? (Who reports what, when do they report it, and to whom and in what formats?)

The answers to these questions should be documented in the project file thus far completed. The templates and formats for reports, the frequency of those reports, and the application of the various metrics should be clear to all stakeholders. It will be up to the project team to adhere to and enforce those standards and metrics throughout the life of the project and to adjust the system to get consistent, timely, quality information to support the decision making required.

It's imperative that the project manager get everyone oriented and motivated. Although the first task could be relatively easy, the second could be a serious challenge. Tools such as a phase kickoff meeting, a team charter, an organization chart, and regular status meetings can help with the orientation. But the fact that project managers often have to coax performance from individuals over whom they have little or no positional power can prove challenging.

Who's On Board, and Why?
Stakeholder Priorities

As we start moving, it's important to note that team members often serve on various project teams simultaneously and have numerous "number one" priorities at the same time. To get the best performance, the project manager must understand and respond to each team member's WIIFM (what's in it for me). Only when this individual motivational perspective is understood can the project manager get optimal performance from the team member. The project manager must also appeal to each project stakeholder's WIIFM to get the very best performance out of each person, whether it be an input to one of the work packages, a deliverable, or an approval. A special group of stakeholders are the customers, both internal and external. They may not all agree on the goals of the project, and they may have other conflicts; for example, those who specialize in financial issues want to keep costs to an absolute minimum, while the end-user customer wants additional functionality or the capacity for future expansion or change in the project.

Keeping the Passengers Happy:
Managing Customer Expectations

Just as a driver will keep passengers informed and calm by advising them of their progress on the trip and telling them when there will be a deviation from the planned route, one of the project manager's principal duties throughout the project is managing customer expectations. While customer expectation management begins at least as early as the requirements definition phase of the project and continues through project closeout, it's especially important during the execution phase. This process starts with the development of clear, documented customer expectations, including the customer acceptance criteria.

The process continues with frequent communications between the project manager and the customer. The project manager must judge the amount and type of communications (status reports, face-to-face meetings, work site visits, etc.) that will meet the customer's needs and make them feel truly included in the management of the project. The project manager will often find it necessary to remind the customer of the agreed-upon requirements, pointing out how the project team is delivering as promised. The project manager should also keep a log of the extras that the team delivers beyond what was agreed upon, because this information will become valuable at the end of the project to counter complaints and/or enhance customer satisfaction. Where problems arise, it's important to keep the customer informed and to ensure that they understand that the team has acted professionally in taking all appropriate steps to deal with those problems. By ensuring that the customer understands the situation, the project manager and team are getting a sort of buy-in from the customer, and when done properly they can have a satisfied customer even when they don't meet all of the project goals. This satisfaction results from the customer's understanding of all that was done and all the obstacles that were overcome to get to this point in the project. But this level of customer satisfaction isn't easily achieved without a conscious on-going effort by the project manager and team. This conscious effort begins with open and frequent communications – and not only about what's going right.

Don't Hide Problems

Problems seldom improve when hidden; they must be brought out into the light. Manure without air just stinks; but brought out into the air and sunlight and properly cultivated, it becomes wonderful fertilizer. So the project manager needs to cultivate problems and challenges so that they become a source of growth for the project and the team. This process starts with the monitoring of all the activities and possible risks of the project and with the prompt reporting of events including precursors to risks (trigger conditions), the actual occurrence of risks, and milestones accomplished or missed. Only when such information is promptly disseminated to all who need to know can you hope to achieve excellence in customer expectation management. The risk register, assumption log, and issue log are three of the principal tools for documenting and tracking these matters (see Exhibit 8-2).

Detours and Revised Routes: Change Management

An area that must often be addressed as part of customer expectation management is the change management process. Customers often want changes in their projects, and some don't like to be constrained by the level of process and documentation required to maintain control of the project scope. For the project manager this is an area where compromise isn't acceptable. The project manager must assure that everyone involved with the project understands and adheres to the change management process. Failure to adhere to the process can result in scope creep (unapproved increases in scope), cost and schedule overruns, undocumented features in the system, and an inaccurate project file. The process includes four elements:

- Documented change management process
- Change control board (change management board and/or configuration management board)
- Change request form (see Exhibit 8-3)
- Project change log (see Exhibits 8-4 and 8-5)

Every change must be submitted on a request form and logged into the system, and then action (acceptance, rejection, or referral) is taken by the change control board. Most changes will have an effect on the project cost or schedule or both. Normally, before a change is accepted, the team must analyze the impacts and determine how it will affect the risk picture.

Risk No.	Risk Description	Category	Potential Impact	Risk Owner	Probability of Occurence (1-5)	Impact of Risk (1-5)	Risk Event Value	Trigger Conditions	Response	Status
R01	Assessor not available	Resource risk	Project delay	Mary A.	1	3	Low	Family obligation		
R02	Lack of team participation	Resource risk	Project incomplete	Bill B.	1	3	Low	Poor project manager		
R03	Inadequate buy-in	Project management risk	Project incomplete	Mary A.	2	4	Medium	No high-level involvement	Mitigate	Under review
R04	Sr. management support nominal	Project management risk	Project failure	Chip C.	1	5	High	No high-level involvement	Mitigate	Under review
R05	Lack of sponsorship	Project management risk	Project failure	Mary A.	2	5	High	No high-level involvement	Mitigate	Mitigated
R06	Change in priorities	Project management risk	Project delay	Mary A.	2	4	Medium			
R07	Results not respected	Project management risk	No value added	Joan K.	2	4	Medium	No high-level involvement		Under review
R08	Pace of progress too slow	Project management risk	Project delay	Joan K.	2	3	Medium	Lack of tracking		
R09	Server downtime	Technical risk	Project delay	Bill B.	3	3	Medium			
R10	Videoconference unavailable	Technical risk	Project delay	Bill B.	3	3	Medium	Overbooked	Mitigate	Mitigated

Exhibit 8-2. Risk Log

151

SCOPE CHANGE REQUEST/IMPACT FORM

Document Preparation Information

PROJECT NAME   PREPARED BY (PRINT)   DATE PREPARED   PROJECT ID   CHG NO.

Proposed Change

BASELINE DESCRIPTION

Give an in-depth explanation of the original system design and architecture. Explain why this was originally the selected solution.

CHANGE DESCRIPTION

Define the product or technical design changes that must be carried out to implement the change request. Identify all WBS elements and work packages affected by the change. If additional resources are required or if resources must be shifted, show the impact on the existing work package implementation.

REASON FOR CHANGE

Describe circumstances resulting in need for change request. Include timing, personnel involved, and summary of the issues.

BUDGET IMPACT

State the cost to complete this change request. Identify and analyze projected financial consequences of making the requested change. Estimate cost differentials as precisely as possible, and include a recommendation on any changes in the customer's obligations.

SCHEDULE IMPACT

State the impact on the project schedule of this change. Include references to the critical path. Discuss workarounds to preserve schedule if possible.

Tasks and Other Information Needed to Complete the Solution

TASK	START DATE	END DATE	DURATION	RESOURCE(S)
Task 1	__/__/__	__/__/__	X days	Resource 1, Resource 2
Task 2	__/__/__	__/__/__	Y days	Resource 1
Task 3	__/__/__	__/__/__	Z days	Resource 3, Resource 4

Authorization – Project Manager

NAME (PRINT)   SIGNATURE   PHONE   DATE

Authorization – Business Sponsor

NAME (PRINT)   SIGNATURE   PHONE   DATE

Exhibit 8-3. Scope Change Request/Impact Form

PROJECT CHANGE LOG

Project Name:

CHG NO.	CHANGE DESCRIPTION	DATE SUBMITTED	DATE CLOSED	DISP CODE*	CHANGE IMPACT**	DURA-TION	RESEARCH HOURS	LABOR HOURS
1								
2								
3								
4								
5								
					Total	___	___	___

*Disposition Code
    A = Change accepted in project
    C = Change rejected or withdrawn
    X = Estimate adjustment

**Change Impact Code
    H = High, extremely important or imperative to change
    M = Medium, important, but we can operate without this change
    L = Low, desirable, but with little impact if the change is not made

Exhibit 8-4. Project Change Log

These considerations will be inputs to the decision on the change request. Depending on the organization, the change control board could have different functions. In some cases they will actually consider each change request and approve, reject, or defer it. In other organizations the board will prioritize changes that have already been approved and will cancel changes that have been preempted by subsequent changes or developments. Many organizations have different levels of change control boards, and for large changes, or for changes to critical projects, the person or group proposing the change may have to run the gauntlet, appearing at increasingly powerful boards, which sometimes may end with an appearance before the board of directors to get final approval.

Occasionally there will be a change where the change request process will take much longer and require more work than implementing the change. This is not a reason to exempt that change from the system. Should a team member not want to burden the customer with the completion of the request, then that team member should complete the request

PROJECT CHANGE LOG INSTRUCTIONS

Purpose

The project change log serves two purposes: it provides a summary record of all the project change requests that have been submitted for the project, regardless of the disposition of the change request; and it serves as a management reference for approved changes in project scope, deliverables, cost, or duration. This log and the scope change request/impact form provide a reference source for both the project manager and the customer or user, keeping them apprised of the change requests and the disposition of those requests.

Origination and Timing

A scope change request/impact form must be completed prior to entering a change request in the project change log. The project manager completes the project change log. The frequency of updating and distributing the project change log is documented in the statement of work. Typically, the change log will be published weekly in conjunction with the project status report.

Forms

- *Project change log:* A project change log template is available.
- *Scope change request/impact form:* A detailed description of a project change request. The scope change request/impact form is completed prior to entering the change in the project change log.

Field Instructions

- *Chg. No.:* The change number is the identification number you assign to the change request when you record a change in the project change log. Use a sequential numbering scheme that you will apply to all changes for the project (beginning with "1" is fine). Enter the change number on the scope change request/impact form in order to cross-reference the change request form with the change log.
- *Change Description:* Briefly describe the change based on the information in the scope change request/impact form.
- *Date Submitted:* Date on which the change request was submitted to the project manager.
- *Date Closed:* Date on which this change request was accepted, rejected, or withdrawn. If accepted, the work and schedule impact of the change should be incorporated in the project plan.
- *Disp.:* The disposition code records the final disposition of the change.
  - A = Change accepted in project
  - C = Change rejected or withdrawn
  - X = On hold or pending

Exhibit 8-5. Project Change Log Instructions

- *Change Impact:* This code indicates the impact of this change on the business group or area:
    - H = High (extremely important or imperative to change)
    - M = Medium (important, but we can operate without this change)
    - L = Low (this change is desirable, but with little impact if the change is not made)
- *Duration:* Enter the estimate for the duration (in days) that this change will add to the project schedule.
- *Research Hours:* Enter the number of hours that will be (or have been) spent to research this change.
- *Labor Hours:* Enter the number of person-hours that this change will add to the project.
- *Total:* As changes are incorporated in the project, calculate the total for each of the impact metrics (duration, research hours, and labor hours).

Exhibit 8-5 continued. Project Change Log Instructions

and submit it to the system. Remember, poor change management is usually one of the top causes of troubled projects. This is an area where the project manager must insist on compliance.

Reserve Fuel: The Change Pot

Some clients pay for each change in a project, but often, whether the client is internal or external, they don't. Where the system doesn't allow for charging the client for the change, there's another tool that helps keep some clients somewhat restrained. That tool is the *change pot.* The change pot is a contingency fund in the project budget to deal with what would otherwise be unfunded changes. This fund is created during the estimating phase or as soon as possible after, and it adds to the project budget the amount of time and/or money that this client's projects, or this type of project, usually go over budget and schedule. So if a certain type of project (or this type of project for the current client) usually experiences a 30-percent cost overrun, the budget has a change pot in that amount added to it. Then, as unfunded changes occur or are proposed, the client is given an estimate of what it will cost to investigate the change. They can then choose to investigate the change or not, with any activity being charged against the change pot. After the change is investigated the client is given an estimated cost for implementation of the change, and they again decide whether they should go forward or not, with any costs being charged against the change pot. While the change pot is sometimes only a paper fund, it has a significant effect on the client, who actually feels that he or she is spending real money. This approach recognizes the reality of cost and schedule overruns and brings the client into an active and informed decision-making position, which clarifies exactly why a project went long or over budget due to unfunded changes.

Checking the Gauges: Status Meetings

One of the most important techniques for keeping project execution on track is to hold regular status meetings with established agendas. By making risk the first item (or at least one of the top three items) on those agendas, the project manager keeps the team focused on the ongoing importance of risk management. The risk portion of the agenda typically involves team members who are assigned to monitor and manage specific risks for the team. Those team members report on their risks if they're among the top five or ten risks during the upcoming work period. After risk reporting, the progress on various milestones is typically discussed. The emphasis should be on very basic questions such as: Are we meeting the schedule and milestones? Are the deliverables meeting all required standards? In conducting these meetings it's essential that the focus be on status reporting, not on problem solving. Should the team identify problems that need solutions, the problem solving should be done in a meeting separate from the status meeting. That meeting can even follow immediately after the status meeting, as long as those who aren't required to be present for the solution meeting are excused.

By not allowing the status meeting to degenerate into a problem-solving meeting, and not keeping team members overtime in meetings, the project manager increases the chance that members will attend status meetings and be prompt. Meeting minutes need to be created and distributed shortly after the meeting, and those on the distribution list for the minutes should have only a few days to challenge the content of the minutes. After that short period the unchallenged minutes should stand as agreed upon. Normally there will also be a project status report on a weekly basis that summarizes the project status and is distributed to project stakeholders and interested senior managers (see Exhibit 8-6).

Steady, Predictable Driving Reduces Accidents!

It's easy to follow a good leader. Like an excellent driver, the project manager follows standard procedures – such as clearly signaling intentions well in advance – and takes action well before critical situations develop. For project leaders one big challenge in dealing with the issues presented during project execution is to react consistently to variation from the standards. Doing so makes it much easier for all who are following their lead. A first step toward this goal is to establish the tolerance for variation for the budget, the schedule, and the scope. Individual milestones may have higher or lower tolerances, and these need to be documented and communicated to the team so that they can monitor for these variations. Teams will normally establish *action parameters* for each item being measured, and should the variation reach that level, action must be taken to deal with the problem. For drivers examples of these parameters include indicators that you need to change lanes or start braking or speed up to deal with a developing situation. For project managers and leaders these parameters will vary from project to project and customer to customer. They can also vary according to the stage of the project, timing in the organization's fiscal cycle, or because of outside influences (such as changing monetary exchange rates).

Whatever the standards, the reaction to similar situations should be consistent. Inconsistent reactions make it much harder for the team members driving behind you to have safe trips or to plan for the future. And when actions are taken they should be documented and communicated to the appropriate stakeholders so that the stakeholders understand how Project Roadtrip is progressing.

REGULAR, CLEAR, AND COMPLETE COMMUNICATIONS are the foundation upon which great project execution relies. The project manager can expect to spend over 80 percent of his or her time communicating. Clear organization, well-defined roles and responsibilities, and the mandatory use

WEEKLY PROJECT STATUS REPORT

TO: (INCLUDE APPROPRIATE ADDRESSEES)

FROM: DIVISION OR BUSINESS UNIT NAME

PROJECT NAME:

STATUS REPORT FOR WEEK ENDING: ___/ ___/ ___

Project Description
Enter a short description of the project and the outcome.

Activities and Accomplishments for Period Ending ___/ ___/ ___
List the week's activities and accomplishments that have been achieved for this project.

Plans for Week Ending ___/ ___/ ___
State the current week's objectives and significant activity for this project.

Target Dates
List any new, changed, or significant target dates.

TASK   TARGET DATE

Assumptions
List any assumptions.

Issues
List any issues (new or open) that require an action plan.

Risks
List any new or continuing risks associated with the project. Always include risks documented in the project charter.

Note: Include the project schedule showing delays to the critical path. Include other project status graphics as necessary to support information in this report.

Exhibit 8-6. Weekly Project Status Report

of various project management tools are ways to achieve that level of communication and documentation that will serve the ends of this project and future projects that rely on its record.

CHAPTER NINE

Monitoring and Controlling the Project

Measuring performance is not as simple as it seems.
— Philip Streatfield, *The Paradox of Control in Organizations*

The root cause of inaccurate status reporting is that PMs are simply not trained to carry out this important activity."
— Capers Jones, *Crosstalk Magazine,* June 2006

QUITE OFTEN project managers believe that monitoring and controlling projects is a relatively straightforward process. However, as the quotes above underscore, it's harder than we think to monitor and control project events. This chapter will discuss some of the underlying reasons why and suggest techniques for monitoring and controlling success.

The Butterfly Effect

The goal of project monitoring is to gain useful information upon which control decisions can be made. But projects are a collection of hundreds or thousands of interacting parts and events. The signs of trouble can often be hidden. We know that when large, damaging events occur on projects, they didn't happen all at once; they began as seemingly minor events that grew and combined over time to become something catastrophic. This problem in projects sounds eerily like the chaos theory concept called the butterfly effect, which is popularly expressed as "a butterfly flapping its wings in South America creates a wind, that eventually grows to become a tornado in Texas." While this may not be literally true, it's descriptive of the way minor events can combine in unforeseen ways to create massive, complex, negative events. This is the same concept that we struggle with on projects. A project assumption left unresolved in planning becomes a major problem in execution. A requirement left to be determined becomes a software defect that threatens the stability of the entire program. Two key concepts for limiting the butterfly effect are: *Have a plan* and *monitor effectively!*

Having a plan means that the project team builds as much of a plan as they can based upon the type of work they're doing. In chaos theory terms, this plan is referred to as the *area of order* (AOO). This AOO is critical to the team's ability to monitor and control the project. It allows the team to identify variance earlier and to start to work on resolving it before it grows to become a project hurricane. This is the concept of *identify early,* which is so important to ensure that as many butterflies as possible are identified as early as possible. This is a challenge because monitoring activities require time and effort, and many project managers believe that time not dedicated to actual work on the project doesn't add value. Additionally, many of the systems or approaches used by organizations to plan, monitor, and control projects don't deliver an adequate level of detail or enough feedback to identify that a butterfly – or, in project management parlance, a variance – is in the system and where it is. Ideally we should establish our area of order early in the project life cycle.

As you can see in Exhibit 9-1, the potential cost of variances increases as the project proceeds through the project life cycle. This fact makes the case that taking time to plan in the front of the project is beneficial.

Monitor Effectively

It's unrealistic to think that a project team can identify and remove all the causes of variance from the project. In fact, the team should *not* automatically act on each occurrence of variance because some variance is normal. However, each occurrence should be examined and understood so that

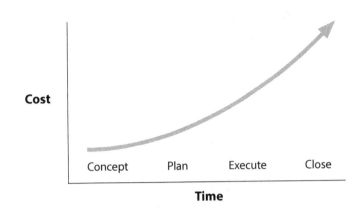

Exhibit 9-1. Potential Impact of the Butterfly Effect
The potential cost of variances increases as the project proceeds through the project life cycle.

proper action will be taken. To ensure that as many variances as possible are revealed, you must implement tools and techniques that collect the right data and are sensitive enough to make you aware of the existence of a variance as soon as possible. Whether you're concerned about variances or just basic project performance for reporting purposes, effective monitoring of the project ensures that the right actions are taken to produce the desired result. Effective monitoring tools should meet these criteria:

- They can be applied consistently throughout the project life cycle
- They are easily understood by their users
- They should be concise
- The data are easy to gather
- Data collected should provide real, actionable information

The Relationship of Monitoring to Controlling

Monitoring is the systematic and organized collection of data to be used to analyze and report project performance and to forecast project result. Controlling is the decisions made and actions taken within the project

163

to influence or regulate the result. These concepts seem simple, yet their misapplication is the root of frequent project problems.

Two things seem to happen nearly simultaneously in project management: the plan is executed, and variation begins to impact it. For this reason our first steps in a project – the WBS and project plan – include specific work activities that we can monitor. Two simple rules to remember are:

◆ The collection of monitoring data for no purpose is a waste of time and a source of unrecoverable cost.

◆ The implementation of control actions not based on data or an understanding of the long-term vision for the project is a perfect example of a fix, as in the expression "today's fix is the beginning of tomorrow's problem." A good conceptual model to keep in mind when monitoring and controlling your project is the *plan, do, check,* and *act* (PDCA) cycle popularized by quality movement guru W. Edwards Deming. This approach, as seen in Exhibit 9-2, is a systematic approach that includes monitoring and control.

The PDCA cycle reminds the project team to define what's to be measured during the planning phase. It also reminds the team that this approach is cyclical – not done just once. And lastly, the PDCA cycle indicates that action is not always necessary, but an organized collection and examination of the data is.

Design of the Monitoring System

There are as many different approaches to performing project management as there are projects. The type of project, its goals, the timeline, the budget, and many other factors cause organizations and project teams to follow various life cycles in accomplishing project work. The first important decision is to define the type(s) of monitoring activities that they want in the project. In general, there are three approaches to monitoring: *in situ* review, phase review, and closure (or end) inspection.

In situ monitoring is the frequent collection of data. It can take place in weekly meetings, daily stand-up reviews, or when project team members review the project data. This process is structured to ensure that key items

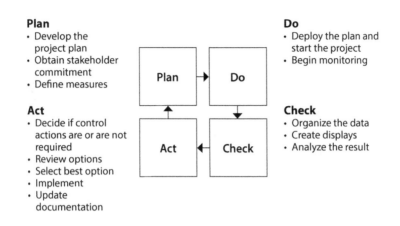

Plan
- Develop the project plan
- Obtain stakeholder commitment
- Define measures

Act
- Decide if control actions are or are not required
- Review options
- Select best option
- Implement
- Update documentation

Do
- Deploy the plan and start the project
- Begin monitoring

Check
- Organize the data
- Create displays
- Analyze the result

Exhibit 9-2. The Plan-Do-Check-Act Cycle
The PDCA cycle reminds the project team to define what is to be measured during the planning phase. It also reminds the team that this approach is cyclical — not done just once.

are reviewed. The *in situ* review is normally conducted by the project manager, project sponsor, or project team.

The second approach to project monitoring, which is more widely practiced, is the phase review. This type of review establishes a review meeting at key points in the project life cycle. Exhibit 9-3 shows an example of a product development life cycle with review points indicated by triangles.

In the process depicted here, the management oversight team is responsible for conducting the phase reviews and for deciding to continue the project, stop it, or delay it for adjustment.

The third type of monitoring system is the closure inspection. This type of monitoring is a collection of data at the end of the project including lessons learned and the result. The closure review is normally conducted by the project sponsor or the project manager. It can also include the customers, key stakeholders, and others whose input is deemed valuable. This type of review should be highly structured to ensure effective, consistent data collection.

One of the criticisms of the closure inspection approach is that the data is collected *too late* to benefit the subject project. Though this is true,

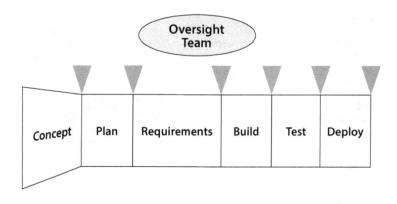

Exhibit 9-3. Phase Review Process
In this example product development life cycle, phase reviews of the project are held at specified review points (indicated by triangles).

most organizations recognize that the purpose of any inspection is to gain knowledge for improvement. The closure inspection data should be used to improve future project performance. An emerging best practice with closure inspection has been to combine it with phase reviews to collect lessons learned specific to each phase. For example, use a closure review as an after-phase item to learn how the organization can write better requirements or perform more effective testing.

The project team should select one, all, or some combination of the monitoring design approaches discussed above. This monitoring system should be implemented consistently across all projects to ensure the orderly collection of project data.

Data Collection Considerations

Experienced project managers know that if data isn't collected in a routine, standardized way, it's of little value. Project organizations need to determine the following for their monitoring systems:

- ◆ What are we trying to know? (criteria)
- ◆ What is the effective measure for that data? (metric)

166

◆ What data should we collect for that measure? (test)

◆ Where can that data be most effectively collected? (monitor)

◆ Who should collect that data? (control)

In many cases organizations will take a somewhat generic approach to project monitoring activities and direct the project team to report simple key data for the project such as:

◆ Schedule status (ahead, behind, on track)

◆ Cost performance (over budget, under budget, on budget)

◆ Scope status (scope changes, test results)

◆ Accomplishments (deliverables completed this reporting period, issues resolved, risk resolved, etc.)

◆ Forecasts (upcoming major deliverables, key activities, project result projections)

◆ Issue or guidance discussion

Whatever approach your team takes for monitoring the project, remember that the consistent collection of data both saves time and enables effective project decision making and improvement.

Data Display

Another consideration for the monitoring process is the display of the collected data. Project data can be displayed in a great many ways. The goal of display is to provide data in a simple, graphic way so that it assists the decision makers with their control activities. Project software can be very helpful in that the software displays (e.g., Gantt charts, network diagrams, resource loading sheets) can be shared and will be consistent for all users of the software. Not all organizations have a standard for the use of one type of software or for data collection. That limits that organization's ability to share information among its parts, to act uniformly on variation, to work effectively with vendors, and to keep useful historical records. It's true that desktop software tools can be used effectively to manage projects, but the use of these tools is often personal in that the

PROJECT DASHBOARD						
Project Name	Schedule	Phase	Start	Finish	% Done	Strategic Goal
B4B Release 12	●	Executing	9/4/05	8/8/06	85%	Customer-based
CDR Facility	●	Closing	1/5/06	9/8/06	98%	Infrastructure
Website Migration	○	Initiating	7/8/06	2/8/07	2%	Infrastructure
PMO Upgrade	●	Executing	6/6/06	4/1/07	20%	Infrastructure
SOX Reporting	●	Executing	3/5/06	8/5/06	80%	Mandatory
Strategic Plan	●	Executing	8/5/06	1/5/07	10%	Mandatory
Risk Assessment	●	Initating	7/5/06	2/2/07	15%	Mandatory
Money Orders	●	Closing	6/6/05	7/1/06	95%	Value-add
CDR-QVC	●	Executing	5/9/06	4/1/07	30%	Environment

Exhibit 9-4. Project Dashboard
Some of the displays used by project teams combine various monitoring tools into one overall "dashboard" for monitoring the project. The project team (or management) identifies the items to track on the dashboard, and if it's linked to project software, the system updates automatically. Schedule status is often communicated visually using green (OK), yellow (some concern), and red (significant issues) graphic displays.

project manager sets it up to his or her standards, which may vary considerably from those of the other project managers in their organization. Some examples of data displays that the project team might consider are shown in Exhibits 9-4 through 9-7.

These tools are a few of the many for monitoring projects. Most organizations have folks with knowledge of statistics and graphics who can help if you're not experienced in this area. Engaging them to help your project team to organize the collected data can often save time and expand your team's understanding and project performance.

Some key considerations for selecting the right display are:

◆ It distills data into a simple, easy-to-understand graphic.

◆ It can be shared easily with key project team members.

◆ It can be understood by the audiences who will view it.

◆ It uses a condensed approach to display (with backups if necessary).

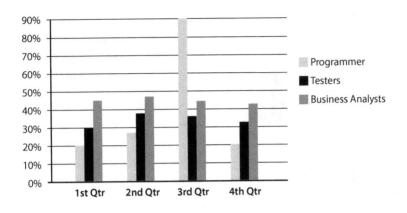

Exhibit 9-5. Resource Bar Chart

The bar chart displays project performance data in a simple-to-read format. In the example above we are examining the percentage of available resource capacity (programmers, testers, and business analysts) obligated in each quarter of a given year. The project team can use this data to determine when more project work can be added or when a resource is overloaded.

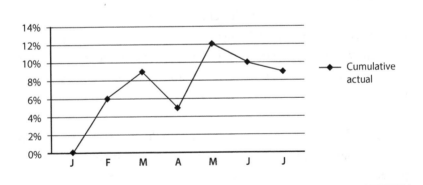

Exhibit 9-6. Percentage over Budget Run Chart

In the run chart above, the project team is able to understand how they are performing in relation to their budget over time. The key here is that they can see trends and act on those trends in order to reverse them, or enhance them if the trend is a positive one (cash savings). In this chart we see that the project is 9% over budget by March. The team took management action, which reduced the overage to 5% in April. Unfortunately that did not completely remedy the problem and in May the overage shot up to 12%.

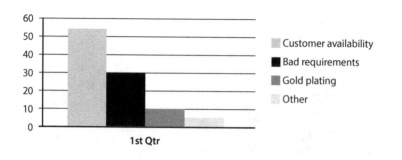

Exhibit 9-7. Pareto Diagram of Defect Causes
The Pareto diagram is also a bar chart, but it's unique because it displays data in descending order of importance or magnitude. This type of diagram can help the project team identify key sources of problems, risks, or major areas of focus.

Earned Value Management

Many of the systems used to manage project performance are limited in that they present data in a single-view format. For example, look at the project budget chart in Exhibit 9-8.

What can we infer from this chart? Are we doing a good job on the project? Are we within the budget projections? We learn very little from this chart without some context and some understanding about other parts of the project. To be effective in monitoring and controlling projects, we need a consistent view of the project that considers the interrelationships of time, cost (resources), scope, and performance.

Earned value management (EVM) provides just such a view. EVM is a system that's more widely used on government and government-related projects, but it's increasingly used by projects outside of the government domain. EVM is "a methodology that combines scope, schedule, and resource measurements to assess project performance and progress" (PMI 2017, p. 705) It has been characterized (though it isn't always) as an objective project measurement and management system. Though many authors make this topic quite complex, it's fundamentally very simple.

For example, suppose you're asked to go on a business trip out of town for two days. You had planned to mow the lawn but you don't get around

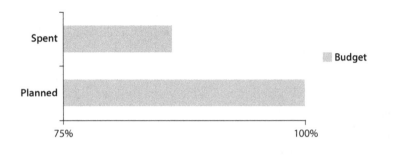

Exhibit 9-8. Project Budget Bar Chart
Single views of data like that shown in this chart often do not provide the information needed to make effective decisions. Are we doing a good job on the project? Are we within the budget projections?

to it. You ask your teenager to mow the front and back lawns. She agrees, and to sweeten the pot you offer $20 ($10 for the front and $10 for the back). Now she's excited: "I'll get started right now!" In a moment of weakness, you give her the $20 up front. You jump into a taxi and leave for the trip. Your child mows the front lawn and stops to take a rest. As she sits on the front porch, one of the passing neighborhood kids invites her to go to the arcade. Your child says, "I have $20!" So away they go. Day turns to night and your child comes home too late to finish the lawn. The next day she just forgets – after all, the $20 is history. When you return home later that day you're disappointed to see that the job isn't complete – the front lawn is finished but the back is still undone.

This simple story helps us to understand the earned value approach because it demonstrates the key concepts. The first factor we're concerned with is *planned value* (PV). PV is the authorized budget assigned to scheduled work. In simpler terms, it's the amount budgeted (normally monetary) to the work that's scheduled to be accomplished (WBS activities or work packages) in the plan *at a given point in time*. In the story above, the PV is $20 ($10 for the front and $10 for the back). In some software systems PV is known as *budgeted cost of work scheduled* (BCWS).

A second important earned value term is *actual cost* (AC). The AC is the realized cost incurred for the work performed on an activity during a specific time period. Again, in easier to understand language, it's the total of the actual costs (normally monetary) expensed or paid out against specific activities and work packages in the project. In the example above, the AC was $20 because you *paid* your child the full amount before you left. Another term for AC is the *actual cost of work performed* (ACWP).

Finally, the key question is: "What value am I getting for my investment?" That factor is known as *earned value* (EV). EV is a measure of the work performed expressed in terms of the budget authorized for that work. In other words, it's work completed valued in monetary terms. In the case above, the EV when you return home is $10 (only half of the work is done). EV is also known as the *budgeted cost of work performed* (BCWP).

These three factors help the project team identify a) what should have been done, b) what has been done, and c) what the value of the work performed is (and thus the value of the project). To extend the ideas of earned value into performance monitoring and forecasting, a few more terms are necessary to discuss:

◆ **Budget at completion (BAC).** This is the sum of all the budgets established for the work to be performed. If you did everything you said you would, when you said you would do it, the cost of all of that without change is the BAC. If there is a change, of course, the BAC should be reviewed.

◆ **Cost performance index (CPI).** This is a key figure for cost monitoring and is normally a fixture of project dashboards. It's a ratio that expresses the cost efficiency for the project. The formula for CPI is EV ÷ AC. In the story above, the EV is $10 and the AC is $20. That yields a CPI of .50. In other words, for every dollar you spent on that lawn mowing work, you received 50 cents worth of work in return. I think you would agree that this is not an acceptable result. This is the kind of insight that the earned value system can give you for your project, a sub-project, work paths, or work packages. It helps you to identify the butterfly earlier in your monitoring activities.

The earned value management system can also be used to understand performance-to-date in key areas. For example, we can derive the *cost vari-*

ance (CV) by using the formula EV – AC. Using this formula, what is the CV for the lawn mowing story above? (EV (10) – AC (20) = -10.) A negative cost variance result normally indicates a less-than-desirable situation. When the value of the work performed is less than the costs paid out for it, this is often referred to as a cost overrun. Ideally the work will be equal to or greater than (positive) the cost. (Wouldn't it be a good situation if we could get the whole lawn mowed for just $10?)

Another concept used by project managers is *schedule variance* (SV). Schedule variance is equal to the EV – PV. In the simple story above, EV (10) – PV (20) = -10, which means that we're behind schedule. This also is not desirable. These simple formulas and concepts for earned value are just the beginning of a larger discussion that's beyond the scope of this work. Refer to the references in the bibliography for additional earned value readings.

A Final Note about Monitoring

Any attempt to monitor project performance will have intended as well as unintended consequences. It's often the unintended consequences that catch project managers by surprise. In the 1920s a series of experiments was run at the Western Electric Hawthorne Plant in Cicero, Illinois. One of the goals of the study was to determine if better lighting improved worker productivity. Basically, the researchers increased lighting, tracked worker performance, and discovered that worker productivity improved. They made other aesthetic improvements and discovered that productivity again improved. To validate their findings they retarded the lighting and discovered, much to their surprise, that productivity improved again. They discovered that it was not the improvement in lighting that was causing the improvement in performance; it was management's interest in and close monitoring of performance that caused the change.

Every organization needs to gather objective information to improve and guide projects. However, the act of collecting data can create fear if it's not done properly. Leaders of organizations and projects that collect data need to recognize the impact that data collection has on the organization and plan to manage that dynamic.

Some key considerations for project managers who want to reduce fear on their projects are:

◆ Maintain an even composure when hearing good results or bad.

◆ Recognize honesty.

◆ Ensure that you review both good and bad projects during monitoring activities.

◆ Recognize that in most cases, "problems in the system are owned by management and not the fault of the worker." (Deming 1993)

Project Control

The concept of control is one of the easiest and one of the more difficult parts of the project management system. It's easy if the planning and monitoring steps were effective; it's difficult if they weren't or if the organization isn't ready for the control actions. The primary goal of control is to regulate the project result: to influence performance to a given end. In the project environment, control is the process of ensuring that the actual performance is in line with the planned performance. When it isn't, control actions are undertaken to get it back in line. Control has always been identified as one of the core activities of management.

It's important to remember that control activities are fed by the monitoring process, and that's where the more complex activities have taken place. Once data are available, the project team reviews the data to determine if current performance is in line with the plan. When it is, project managers can say that the project is in control (achieving planned results). When it isn't, then control actions may be necessary. There's variation in everything and the key to control is to identify when the amount of variation or the trend of the variation is unacceptable. It's especially a challenge in an interdependent system to consider control actions in view of the whole. In some cases today's control action is tomorrow's variation. Control considerations are depicted in Exhibit 9-9.

Using the control action matrix, when a variance falls into the "Immediate action required" quadrant, the variation has reached unacceptable levels and immediate action is appropriate.

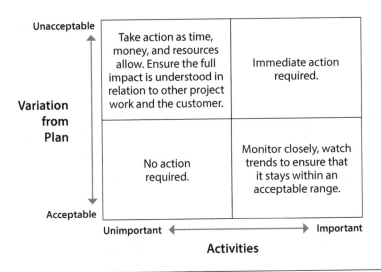

Exhibit 9-9. Control Action Matrix
When a variance falls into the "Immediate action required" quadrant, the variation has reached unacceptable levels and immediate action is appropriate.

Schedule

When key schedule dates are in jeopardy or already late, consider the following actions:

- Fast track (perform tasks in parallel).
- Crash (add resources to a task to speed up its performance).
- De-scope the project (delete or amend some of the planned scope).
- Replan the project (start anew).
- Use resource strategies that gain time (employ higher-level expertise, outsource, etc.).

Cost

The project budget is in jeopardy or already over-obligated. Consider the following actions:

- Seek additional funding from management.

- Consider cost-saving measures such as bundling (grouping services from one provider to obtain price reductions).

- Examine labor profile; consider using lower-cost labor where possible.

- Outsource (outsourced organizations can often have a more economic and efficient approach or knowledge that saves time).

- Use net present value management concepts (delay money out of the project, accelerate customer money into the project).

Scope

The sum of the project's products, services, and results is in jeopardy. If it appears as though you can't deliver all or some of the scope, consider the following actions:

- Renegotiate with the customer and suggest that some scope be moved to a follow-on release of the product, service, or result.

- Delete some of the features and functions.

- Engage additional resources to work on the project.

- Consider outsourcing some of the work.

- Eliminate time off project for key resources, especially those at less than 100 percent utilization.

All control actions should be documented as appropriate.

YOUR PROJECT HAS BEEN INITIATED, planned, executed, and monitored and controlled – now it's time to close it out.

CHAPTER TEN

Closing the Project

IMAGINE THIS: You're a project manager for Digital Mind Manufacturing, a startup software development company. You have several projects currently in progress, including one to improve the manufacturing resource planning software of a highly valued customer. The project has been long and interesting, the deliverables are done, and it's now time to close the project. You meet with the customer and hand over the revised software. The customer is delighted with the final deliverable and accepts ownership of it. The CEO of your firm is also delighted with the result; there is a big handshake and an article in the corporate newspaper about the customer, your work, and the new software. However, with all the excitement and activity surrounding the end of this project, you only had time for a quick team meeting to thank the team members and then a short off-site celebration. You turn your attention to your other projects and the new projects you were being handed as a reward for your good work.

Then the problems begin.

◆ Approximately one month after delivery of the software, the customer is calling for the source code. You're unsure what the contract says in this area and you promise to get back to him.

◆ You receive a call from your finance department; they want to know why you've been billed for $767.23 in long distance phone calls from the phone that's in the office at the client site, *after* you had stopped using that office? (Darn it! You should have shut that phone off!)

◆ Your program manager has informed you that he wants to know the value realization of that MRP project. Regrettably, you didn't do a financial close-out and may not be able to accurately determine that information. You also realize that the program manager is a bulldog and will call you every week until he gets an answer.

◆ The customer is now calling to ask less subtly about the source code, and now also wants you to come out and do some fine-tuning to the user interface. (You wonder if you should be doing this. Isn't this change management? Where's that darn contract?)

◆ It's now two months after delivery, and the finance department is asking why the outsourced vendor on the MRP project is still billing against that project. Did you forget to notify the vendor that the project was over?

◆ The customer is now alleging that you didn't prepare them adequately to work with the new software program and they're demanding on-site training as well as associated materials. Was training included in the contract? Is this new work?

◆ You agree to make some minor improvements to the software for the customer but soon realize that all your programmer assets are assigned 100 percent and in order to help the customer you'll have to set back other projects, and regrettably this will be uncompensated work. Also, if you do this, will the customer expect other free services?

Regrettably, project managers encounter many of the negative outcomes identified above every day. If the closing of a project is not deliberate and planned, you may end up dealing with after-effects and related problems for a long time. In some cases project managers are still trying to resolve issues that are years old! For project managers these sorts of problems can be especially problematic because:

- It's your name that's associated with that project, and you get a lot of unwanted notoriety.

- As indicated in the story above, you're being assigned new projects and these lingering issues divert your attention and energy.

- A lot of good project work can be overshadowed by one or two seemingly insignificant but lingering project closeout issues. (The project manager who left the phone on managed a project that generated over $500,000 in profits, but when he sees his manager, the manager asks, "How could you forget to shut that phone off?")

- A poor finish to the project can reflect very poorly on your firm and lose future business.

Luckily, these and other problems can be prevented by ensuring that your projects are closed using a defined and structured process. The benefits of using a standardized and structured process for closing a project are:

- All the right actions are taken

- Ability to track and manage the benefits and costs of the project (measure value realization)

- More effective management and control of costs, especially the life cycle costs of the deliverables

- Improved stakeholder and customer satisfaction – all stakeholders will know that the project work is concluded and the deliverables have been transferred; therefore, all work from this point forward is baseline management or warranty work and should be handled accordingly

- Better organizational learning because your project team will have an opportunity to reflect on the lessons they've learned and suggest future improvements

◆ A sense of closure and achievement for the team

◆ Improved morale through participation in the closeout process

◆ Improved future performance

A very important note about closeout is that often it's perceived to be a one-time event that occurs at the end of the project. A new, better practice is to conduct a closeout at interim points in the project. For example, as one phase of the project work concludes, before you start the work or get too invested in the next phase, take a moment with your team or your customer and review the previous phase and conduct a closeout meeting for that phase in which you capture lessons learned and opportunities for continuous improvement. This is a current best practice used in many organizations. Don't wait until the last moment to get things done; doing it incrementally makes the process richer and more effective.

Types of Project Closeouts

There are generally two types of project closeouts. The normal closeout is associated with a project that has successfully run its course, has been delivered to the customer, and now must be closed. Most closeouts should be of this type, but for many reasons some are not.

A second type of closeout is the project termination closeout. In this case, for varying reasons (competitive, performance results, environmental), the project is being closed without conclusion. This may also be called premature termination. As an example of this type of closure, an organization created a product, but the final project commercialization review revealed that two competitors were in the marketplace and, as a result of the long developmental time for this project, this product was not substantially better than those on the market already. The Strategic Oversight Team decided to not go commercial with the product and it was retained as an internal tool.

Another example is that of a company that created software for a state government. They were in late-stage development for the product when the state legislature enacted legislation that required a significant amount of rework on the product. The cost of the rework would have been prohibitively higher than starting from scratch. As a result the software company and the state mutually agreed to close the current project and to start again with a new project.

Another important point is that closeout for projects that are conducted internally (no customers outside of your company) aren't conducted with the same discipline as those that are under contract with external customers. This can lead to several key problems:

- Customers continue to place demands on the project team because they don't think that the project is finished.

- Resources cannot be reassigned because they're still receiving work on the old project.

- There's a lack of accomplishment because some projects, like zombies, either never die or continue to come back to life time and time again.

To be effective, every project should go through a formal closeout process. Let's walk through the key closeout activities.

Closeout Activities

Every project and every project environment will require its own unique closeout activities, but there are key activities and systems that are common to many projects. When attempting to identify the items that apply to your project it may be helpful to use a checklist. In his wonderful book *Checklist Manifesto,* author Atul Gawande (2010) makes the case that anyone who is confronted with a complex set of activities can make their work more efficient and effective if they follow a checklist. Closing projects is a prime example of this concept. There are typically so many things that the project manager and team need to ensure that they get done, that a closeout checklist is an indispensable tool to ensure that closeout is done right. Additionally, as mentioned above, it's a good practice to establish a standardized (consistent) process for the closure of a project to make sure that the key things get done and that project performers understand what's required of them. In some organizations project managers have made the checklist items tasks or work packages on their work breakdown structures. It's also important to note that when the requirements of the project are being defined or specified, the work that must be done to complete the project is also being defined. Experienced project managers often say that when you define the deliverables in planning the project, you're defining project closeout requirements as well.

Some of the typical activities found on many project closeout checklists are discussed below. More are listed in Exhibit 10-1.

Contract Closure

Have the responsibilities of each party been met as detailed in the statement of work? If there are remaining work items, have appropriate steps been taken to identify and engage resources to ensure their accomplishment? If the contract has been fulfilled, then take appropriate action (meeting, mail, etc.) to notify the customer about project closure and completion of the contract requirements.

Documentation

Are all relevant document systems completed and closed? Example systems are:

- Scope specification
- Project change log
- Project repository (also known as the project control or project workbook)
- Risk management documents
- Quality management plan (quality assurance and quality control documents)
- System maintenance logs and records

Security

Ensure that the following security-related tasks are performed:

- Temporary access to systems is canceled by system administrators.
- Security badges are collected.

PROJECT CLOSEOUT CHECKLIST				
Item	Task Description	Required		Comments
#		Y	N	
	Closeout delivery			
	Close contract			
	Redeploy people			
	Redeploy assets			
	Settle supplier contracts			
	Perform financial closure • Audit timesheet entries • Act on timesheet audit • Final timesheet printout • Prepare final GP Analysis • Notify accounting to lock time recording system			
	Package final solution results • Prepare archive CDs of project deliverables (one for customer, one for project files)			
	Request customer feedback • Customer satisfaction survey			
	Activate solution support • Set up support contract (where applicable) • Inform customer of support policy			
	Evaluate solution			
	Form evaluation team			
	Evaluate solution components • Quality (meets requirements) • Customer satisfaction • Skills developed • Reusable components • Profitability • Actual schedule			
	Nominate intellectual capital for capture in corporate knowledge management system • Methodologies • Techniques • Skills • Architecture • Industry knowledge • Customer information • Competitive edges • Unique concepts			
	Provide performance feedback			
	Create project completion report			
	(continued)			

Exhibit 10-1. Project Closeout Checklist

183

Item	Task Description	Required		Comments
#		Y	N	
	PROJECT CLOSEOUT CHECKLIST			
	Review and act on evaluation feedback • Adjust techniques and methodologies • Skills development plans • Lunch & learn to share lessons learned			
	Interactive media closure			
	Return collateral to customer			
	Archive source files on CD			
	Organize project files for archive • PCB (hardcopy) • Email database • Archive correspondence			
	Get project reference approval			
	Get approval to enter project into competitions			
	Prepare marketing brief			
	Post referencable projects in marketing database			
	Post competition-able projects in marketing database			
	Prepare public relations announcements • Lunch & learn • Company-wide memos • Management briefing			
	Recognize team contribution			
	Other completion items			
	Prepare final report to customer • Financial results • Schedule results • Quality results			
	Verify and document compliance with all contractual terms			
	Compile customer acceptance documents			
	Initiate and pursue claims against customer			
	Prepare and conduct defense against claims by customer			
	Identify new business and enter into lead capture system or process as contract extensions (PCRs) • Project extensions • New business			
	Update accounting records to show project closed			

Exhibit 10-1 continued. Project Closeout Checklist

- Unique accounts such as Outlook access are cancelled.
- Physical security is notified of status change.
- Key corporate information is returned.

Financial

To understand the financial performance of the project, validate value realization. To ensure that charges to the project are concluded, consider the following actions:

- Close out charge codes (unique codes assigned to the project against which project charges are recorded; these charge codes help to track expenses and charges to projects).
- Prepare final project financial report.
- Check to ensure that all financial obligations have been met and all expenses have been paid.

Vendor/Contractor

In many cases contracts with vendors or contractors require a formal written notice of project close. Ensure that you understand the provisions of the contract that you're using and comply with its provisions. Some typical activities to consider are:

- Notify the vendor/contractor of the final date for billing.
- Ensure that the vendor/contractor is aware of and has a plan to complete any items for which they're responsible that are not yet completed.
- Prepare the required vendor/contractor performance reports for your procurement department.
- Prepare the vendor/contractor feedback/performance report.
- Pay the final vendor/contractor charges (keep retainage, or set aside contingency money from contractor payments when appropriate).

Legal

For many projects there are legal considerations. Consider a legal review of project documentation to ensure that unique corporate confidential information is identified and managed accordingly. Also, review key documents to identify intellectual property, and manage those in accordance with your corporation's IP directives.

Benefits Management

This is an emerging area of importance. Many organizations undertake projects to achieve the results predicted in the business case or the program or project charter. However, historically, those same organizations have done a poor job at measuring and tracking to ensure that those promises were achieved after the investment is complete. Benefits closeout will probably require some measurement at the start of the project and some measurement at the close of the project. Additionally, it may require actions to continue the measurement system after the project has closed. The project manager and the team need to plan for this important action as appropriate.

Logistics

This area may not affect every project, but it's worthy of consideration on enough projects that it's mentioned here.

- Return leased, rented, or borrowed materials and equipment.
- End office and workspace rental agreements.
- End rented or leased living arrangements.
- Document and return corporate assets. Include loans of equipment or software between stakeholders. Many organizations have property that must be signed for when borrowed; ensure that all material is returned and that you're released from responsibility.

Customer

This is perhaps the most sensitive area of the closeout process. Even if the project has gone well it can break down in the end if closeout is handled poorly. In those cases where the relationship with the customer has been strained, closeout can be far more challenging and may require unique strategies to deal with such issues as acceptance sign-off and problem resolution. Some of the key activities in any case may be:

◆ Obtain customer satisfaction feedback.

◆ Formally notify the customer of the end date of the project.

◆ Conduct customer acceptance tests.

◆ Deliver key documentation (such as as-built drawings, source code when appropriate, training manuals, help desk info, and warranty info).

Transition

In many cases, to end your responsibility for a project you're required to ensure that the next step in the chain internally or externally is prepared for and accepts responsibility for ownership or management of the project result. Consider the following:

◆ Develop a transition plan.

◆ Activate the warranty.

◆ Turn over maintenance records and instructions.

◆ Conduct a transition meeting when appropriate. This is especially important to ensure the orderly transfer of knowledge.

◆ Communicate the transfer of responsibility widely to ensure that all stakeholders are aware of the new responsible party.

◆ Establish a help desk when appropriate.

◆ Update materials with new operating guidelines. Ensure that business processes have been updated to conform to the project results. This process should have started and been an integral part of the requirements gathering, project design, and implementation. Sarbanes-Oxley and other regulatory environments have made documentation ever more important.

Communication

To ensure that the project is recognized as closed, to advertise key aspects of the project, and to ensure that key stakeholders are aware of changes in responsibilities, some or all of the following steps should be considered:

- Advertise the success of the project and its launch in internal corporate communications vehicles.

- Communicate project closure via several channels.

- Conduct a closeout meeting with team members.

- Conduct a closeout meeting with customers.

- Conduct a closeout meeting with management.

Team Closeout

Perhaps the one closeout area that's accomplished with regularity is team closeout. Project managers often have a need for closure as do many of their project team members. You need to ensure that all recognize that this effort is concluded and that their work is finished, and you want to recognize their contributions and achievements. *Even if a project is terminated early, it's a good practice to conduct a closeout meeting.*

When a project ends prematurely rumors abound, including the belief that there was a negative reason for the project's end. A good team closeout for even terminated projects will give the project manager a chance to ensure that team members recognize that it wasn't their fault that the project ended and to thank them for their good work. For successful and unsuccessful projects the following closeout items should be considered:

- Conduct a team closeout meeting (or celebration meeting if appropriate).

- Notify functional managers or resource managers that the work on the project is complete and their resources are returned (provide the effective date).

- Prepare performance appraisals when appropriate.

- Recognize those resources who performed above and beyond expectations.

◆ Make arrangements to help those resources in need of special help to improve their skills or to enhance their performance.

◆ Record newly acquired skills in the master skills database.

◆ Conduct a lessons learned session. Capture things done well and things that could be done better.

◆ Ensure that internal resources are aware of any remaining work they own.

◆ Document training for team members' professional development files.

Final Thoughts on Project Closeout

The project manager, the project team, and ultimately the organization can increase their abilities, knowledge, and effectiveness by conducting an effective closeout process. However, in many organizations each project is treated as a separate entity unrelated to other projects. In those organizations closeout information from each project isn't compared with the information from other projects. If lessons learned are documented but no action is ever taken, then they're just lessons observed. Those organizations and teams lose a lot of opportunities for learning, improvement, and growth. A growing best practice is the use of a central organization, such as a project office, to collect, organize, and analyze project data. That organization further defines changes to organizational or project practices as a result of the analysis. If a project office doesn't exist in your organization then consider accomplishing these actions at the program or multi-project leadership level. Some excellent ideas for improvement can emerge from this process because improvements in performance are based on objective information collected in a standardized manner.

Another key concern is the trend toward less formality in project management and the perception that the elimination of project bureaucracy speeds performance. If a project is a unique event that will *never* be repeated (in fact or in form) and will also never have to integrate with other projects or events, then, yes, much of the bureaucracy and formality can be eliminated. However, very few projects fit into that narrow parameter.

Most will be revisited for upgrade or improvement or will be done again for a similar purpose. In order to improve project and product production effectiveness we need to gather data and study results to enable enduring improvement in performance through the reduction of rework and scrap. If we don't do this in a routine way we'll become stagnant and ineffective.

Finally, the cataloguing of lessons learned (gathered at different points in the project and not just at the end) should be closely managed. Effective cataloguing of lessons learned requires version control, bookmarks, and effective management. The audience should also be considered and an appropriate method of collection and display selected (for example, having a shared drive on a server that can be accessed remotely is a good idea when the team is geographically dispersed). In fact, the management of lessons learned data is so important that we've devoted an entire chapter to the subject.

YOUR PROJECT HAS BEEN OFFICIALLY CLOSED, but there's one more activity you need to undertake to improve your future project management performance – document your lessons learned.

CHAPTER ELEVEN

Lessons Learned . . . And Used

LESSONS LEARNED are the result of analyzing things that went well (and why) and things that did not go well (and why) in a project. They must be gathered and disseminated as they come to light, not only at the close of the project. Some teams focus heavily on what went wrong and fail to note the successful activities and approaches that they want to replicate in similar future work. The implementation of lessons-learned processes is one of the most important ways to improve the project success rate. A common saying that sums up this concept is "feedback – the breakfast of champions."

Yet until recently lessons-learned processes were unevenly applied, and it's still rare to find an organization that makes full use of the intellectual capital represented by the lessons learned on projects. Why do most projects fall down in the collection of lessons learned? Is it a lack of time, a lack of resources, or a lack of value perceived? Sadly, it's usually all three. Typically the collection of this information occurs at the end of a phase or a project; the people involved may have already moved on to another project, or may be so multi-tasked that they're just happy to accomplish the phase or the project delivery. Further, there's often little immediate reward for doing a good job on lessons-learned collection and documentation. How does one turn this problem around? How is the situation developed where everyone follows a set process and reports lessons learned as early as possible?

Establishing a Lessons-Learned Methodology

The key to success is to establish a lessons-learned methodology early in the project and to get all the stakeholders involved. That means developing:

◆ A written methodology

◆ A standard format for reporting lessons learned

◆ An archive of those lessons learned that's easily accessible by everyone who needs the information

One of the real challenges is getting all stakeholders to adhere to this and the other methodologies used to manage the project, especially if the project manager doesn't have any direct authority over a stakeholder.

The lessons-learned methodology must first lay out the various ways that the lessons learned may be discovered. These should include both inadvertent discoveries and those coming out of formal project reviews as well as ad hoc activities that rely on the expertise of the team members. The formal project reviews must include project status reviews, design reviews, and process reviews. They will compare the then-current state against the project plan and standard work approaches. Project status reviews are normally held on a regular basis (typically weekly, bi-weekly, or monthly depending on the project size, complexity, speed, and criticality), and the reviews monitor and discuss issues such as cost, schedule, scope, and performance. Design reviews typically try to answer the question: does the product, service, or software design meet the requirements that have been defined in the project? Process reviews focus on the question of whether the process can be improved.

The methodology must also provide for discovery of lessons learned outside of formal reviews, such as a problem or noteworthy success that arises during the normal course of business – the discovery of a delay or failure as it occurs. This information should be detailed enough to give all team members awareness of how they may discover a lesson learned so that all will have a better chance of knowing what to look for and of discovering those items or conditions. The issues that merit inclusion in this system are wide-ranging. While matters such as supplier issues, process issues, and technical issues are normally included in most lessons-learned systems, ones often ignored are people issues, including feelings. Because virtually all progress on projects is the result of human effort, one must not give short shrift to the people issues, including feelings and perceptions. Remember that perception is reality for each individual. So deal with those feelings and perceptions, or be plagued by them!

The methodology should then detail how and when the discovered information should be documented. It's best if the information is documented as soon as possible after the event. Requiring that it occur within 24 hours of the event is usually reasonable. There are three reasons for this rapid recording mandate. First, the people involved with the event are still around to remember and document it; second, the passing of time has not skewed memories; and third, rapid recording provides an opportunity for earlier application of the lesson learned. It's critical that the method of documenting should not be so onerous that it's avoided. To deal with that issue, many teams have found that a quick and simple memo or email report serves them very well. The email is favored by most teams because it's their most common form of written communication and because it can usually be forwarded most easily to those with a need to know. The report of the event providing the lesson learned should include seven or eight basic pieces of information about the event. They are:

- ◆ Title of the event (normally selected from a dropdown menu, e.g., Integration Testing Failure)

- ◆ Additional descriptive language about the event

- ◆ The WBS number or some other simple reference number to quickly locate where the work is detailed in the project documentation

- ◆ What happened

- ◆ What the project plan said to do about it

◆ What was really done about it

◆ How the action worked

◆ What the recommendations are for next time

If the description for each item is limited to not more than two sentences, then the report remains manageable. If the report format is designed as a template that can be readily downloaded to a lessons-learned database after review by the team, then the entire step of writing up the lessons learned is moved out of that end-of-phase or end-of-project time period where time and resources are short. Some of the most effective systems use a template with a dropdown menu for the title of the event. By using a dropdown menu, the system forces the original lessons-learned author to classify the event using standardized terminology that will later be more easily searched than if each author could use his or her preferred (and usually non-standard) descriptors for the event. This standardized language and search capability add great value and functionality to the database.

Once the reports are received by the project manager, there must be a process for their immediate review, sometimes with a request for more information or clarification from the reporting party. The reports are forwarded to those who need the information and then archived until the periodic review (at the end of the phase or end of the project) determines which lessons learned finally go into the lessons-learned database for long-term retention and availability.

Should you not have the advantage of gathering lessons-learned ideas from some form of regular reporting such as described above, you could employ a questionnaire (such as in Exhibit 11-1) to elicit some of the most important lessons learned. In addition to the operational facts type of lessons learned described above, many opportunities for lessons learned can be developed by a survey of the project team members. While the survey may seem a very subjective tool, it's vital in order to understand the perceptions of the team members so that project managers can improve their approach, address the concerns and perceptions of team members, and be more cognizant of how others see them and their actions.

Team surveys such the one in Exhibit 11-2 can be done periodically throughout the project to gain insight into team members' feelings and

PROJECT LESSONS LEARNED QUESTIONNAIRE

The purpose of this questionnaire is to help review the results from the project and to translate those results into lessons learned and recommendations for improvement. Attach this document to the project closeout report.

General Questions

- Are you proud of our finished product or system?
- What was the single most frustrating part of our project?
- How would you do things differently next time to avoid this frustration?
- What was the most gratifying or professionally satisfying part of the project?
- Did the Project Management Methodology work? Which of our methods or processes worked particularly well?
- Which of our methods or processes were difficult or frustrating to use? What could be done to improve the process?

Intergroup Coordination

- What difficulty did we have in working with other stakeholders who were responsible for a task or set of tasks relating to the project?
- Did we have the right people assigned to all project roles? Consider subject matter expertise, technical contributions, management, review and approval, and other key roles. If no, how can we make sure that we get the right people next time?
- Did stakeholders, senior managers, customers, and project sponsor(s) participate effectively? If not, how could we improve participation?
- List team members or stakeholders who were missing from the kickoff meeting or who were not involved early enough in our project. How can we avoid these oversights in the future?

Requirements Definition

- Did our requirements definition identify all the project deliverables that we eventually had to build? Did the delivered product meet the specified requirements and goals of the project? If not, what did we miss and how can we be sure to capture necessary requirements on future projects?
- Did our requirements definition mistakenly identify deliverables that were unnecessary? If so, how can we avoid this in the future?

Planning

- Were all team/stakeholder roles and responsibilities clearly delineated and communicated? If not, how could we have improved these?
- Were deliverables specifications, milestones, and specific schedule elements/dates clearly communicated? If not, how could we improve this?

(continued)

Exhibit 11-1. Project Lessons Learned Questionnaire

- Was the Project Budget met? How accurate were our original estimates of the size and effort of our project? What did we over- or under-estimate? Consider deliverables, effort, and materials required.
- Describe any early warning signs of problems that occurred later in the project. How should we have reacted to these signs? How can we be sure to notice these early warning signs next time?
- Were risks identified and mitigated?
- Could we have completed this project without one or more of our vendors/contractors? If so, how?
- Were our constraints, limitations, and requirements made clear to all vendors/contractors from the beginning? If not, how could we have improved our RFP or statement of need?
- Were there any difficulties setting up vendor paperwork (purchase orders, contracts, etc.)? How could these have been avoided?

Executing and Controlling

- Did key team members have creative input into the creation of the design specifications? If not, whom were we missing and how can we assure their involvement next time?
- Did those who reviewed the design specifications provide timely and meaningful input? If not, how could we have improved their involvement and the quality of their contributions?
- How could we have improved our work process for creating deliverables specifications?
- Were the members of our test group truly representative of our target audience? If not, how could we assure better representation in the future?
- Did the test facilities, equipment, materials, and support people help to make the test an accurate representation of how the deliverables will be used in the "real world?" If not, how could we have improved on these items?
- Did we get timely, high-quality feedback about how we might improve our deliverables? If not, how could we get better feedback in the future?
- Was our implementation strategy accurate and effective? How could we improve this strategy?
- Were our status reports produced on time? Were they helpful in monitoring the project? If not, why not?
- What worked well in the review and approval process?
- How did the process for managing change perform?
- Did our hand-off of deliverables to the customer represent a smooth and easy transition? If not, how could we have improved this process?

Exhibit 11-1 continued. Project Lessons Learned Questionnaire

TEAM QUESTIONNAIRE FOR CAPTURING LESSONS LEARNED

Give a rating for each question according to the legend.

Personal
0 = DON'T KNOW 1 = STRONG NO 2 = NO 3 = MIXED OPINION 4 = YES 5 = STRONG YES

- Did you enjoy working on the project?
- Do you feel you have developed additional skills?
- Did you have the necessary skills to meet your objectives?
- Was the training on the project adequate?
- Did you find the work challenging/interesting?
- Additional comments:

Standards
0 = DON'T KNOW 1 = DETRIMENTAL TO THE PROJECT 2 = LITTLE VALUE 3 = SOME USE
4 = VERY USEFUL 5 = EXCELLENT

- Rate the value for the following standards:
  - Documentation standards
  - Turnover procedures
  - Status reports
  - Project walk-throughs
  - Team walk-throughs of subsystems
  - Project management standards and methodology
  - Other (please specify)
- Do you feel the standards were generally adhered to? Yes/No
- What additional standards should the project have developed?
- Additional comments:

Project/Product Development Environment
0 = DON'T KNOW 1 = STRONG NO 2 = NO 3 = MIXED OPINION 4 = YES 5 = STRONG YES

- Did you have the proper equipment needed for the project?
- Did you have adequate software to do your work?
- Were the tools and utilities useful? If not, why?
- Was the office environment good to work in?
- Do you feel the recommended technical solution was a good choice?
- Additional comments:

Development
0 = DON'T KNOW 1 = STRONG NO 2 = NO 3 = MIXED OPINION 4 = YES 5 = STRONG YES

- Was the overall business design clear to you?
- Was the overall technical design clear to you?

Exhibit 11-2. Team Questionnaire for Capturing Lessons Learned

- Did you know where to find documentation on the business and technical designs?
- Was the level of documentation on the project adequate?
- Was the documentation handled in a well-structured manner?
- What procedures/methods would you use again?
- What procedures/methods would you *not* use again?
- Additional comments:

Testing
0 = DON'T KNOW   1 = FAILURE   2 = NEITHER FAILURE NOR SUCCESS   3 = LIMITED SUCCESS
4 = SUCCESSFUL   5 = VERY SUCCESSFUL

- How well do you think the following was handled?
  - System testing -Turnovers
  - Defect reporting/fixing
  - Issues reporting/fixing
- Additional comments:

Communication
0 = DON'T KNOW   1 = FAILURE   2 = NEITHER FAILURE NOR SUCCESS   3 = LIMITED SUCCESS
4 = SUCCESSFUL   5 = VERY SUCCESSFUL

- How successful/useful was the communication?
  - Between colleagues?
  - Between you and your direct supervisor?
  - Between you and the project manager?
  - Between you and the customer?
  - On overall project status?
  - On the objectives of the project?
  - On your objectives?
  - On your performance?
  - On the objectives of the development team?
  - On project decisions?
  - On project issues?
  - On team issues?
- Additional comments:

Planning/Scheduling/Status Reporting
0 = DON'T KNOW   1 = FAILURE   2 = NEITHER FAILURE NOR SUCCESS   3 = LIMITED SUCCESS
4 = SUCCESSFUL   5 = VERY SUCCESSFUL

- How would you rate the overall project planning?
- How would you rate the overall project scheduling?

(continued)

Exhibit 11-2 continued. Team Questionnaire for Capturing Lessons Learned

- Was it difficult to meet deadlines?
- Did you feel involved enough in planning/scheduling?
- Did you feel involved enough in estimation of your work?
- Did you feel comfortable in raising issues?
- Were issues you raised dealt with adequately?
- Did you feel the hours you worked were too long?
- If you worked long hours, did you feel pressured into it?
- Additional comments:

Methodologies
- In your opinion, what methodologies did the project use?
- How well did they work?
- Why?
- Additional comments:

Summary
- What in your opinion were the three main project strengths?
- What in your opinion were the three main project weaknesses?
- In your opinion, was enough attention paid to quality in both the development process and the final product?
- Any other comments you would like to add?

THANK YOU!
Your input is valuable. It will enable us make improvements in future projects.

Exhibit 11-2 continued. Team Questionnaire for Capturing Lessons Learned

perceptions. This can provide an opportunity to correct problems and to support continuous improvement in both process and human relations aspects. The project manager must create and maintain an atmosphere of trust and open communication to be truly successful and to get optimal results from such surveys. Remember, perception is reality!

Don't Shoot the Messenger

A discussion of this issue would not be complete without addressing some of the political and legal realities that one must face. The issue of access to lessons-learned archives creates some problems because lessons learned in many projects may be company confidential, not to be accessed by clients or vendors. This might necessitate having a special company-confidential lessons-learned database in addition to the standard lessons-learned database for the project. Should one have the need to establish this company-confidential record, it's imperative that corporate counsel be consulted on whether or not to do so, and if so, how. Remember, very few writings can be protected from discovery in a legal proceeding.

Another political or cultural issue is how lessons learned are communicated to others. Problems arise when the information needs to cross fence lines from one department or division to another. In many companies different divisions use different project management software tools or methodologies, so there's an initial cultural bias against ideas or lessons learned from other groups. Sometimes the solution or preventive step documented by one group won't work in the other organization, and this problem is only worsened by the global aspects of many projects. A solution that will work in one country may be contrary to law or common practice in another.

One regional project management office of a global organization found it particularly valuable to have a monthly lessons-learned meeting, lasting a couple of hours, that all project managers were required to attend either in person or via teleconference. The goal of this meeting was to provide all project managers with the most up-to-date information on lessons learned on recent projects. This strategy has been tremendously successful for them, even though they have projects underway in five countries. One of the most important benefits of this process has been the more rapid employment of the lessons learned. Instead of waiting until a project has ended and the lessons learned are reviewed and downloaded to the knowledge management database, lessons learned can be acted upon immediately by project managers in other similar projects, thereby saving time and money and impressing clients with the mid-process improvements and cost and schedule savings that the company is able to bring to bear.

While most project managers complain about how many meetings they must attend, this lessons-learned monthly meeting sponsored by the project management office gets nothing but kudos and enthusiastic participation from all of the project managers in that region. They also credit those meetings (along with several other initiatives that they have undertaken, such as their enforcement of compliance with the project management methodology and knowledge management database fulfillment) for their Level 3 rating in project management maturity and improved profitability.

Project managers should apply this same principle by sharing lessons learned at the regular project status meetings and not wait until the end of a project phase or the end of the project to communicate these to the team members and other stakeholders.

Knowledge management systems are entangled with the resolution of the information distribution problem. Availability, habits of use, and ease of use are all foundation questions when one tries to get lessons-learned information disseminated. One of the most effective ways to achieve compliance with use mandates is to incorporate a metric in the project management system and then enforce it. Excellent results have been achieved where project and program managers regularly review the lessons learned and where they have established performance review criteria that measure compliance with the lessons learned and process improvement systems. What gets measured, gets done! So project managers and teams need to find a way to incorporate those performance standards and measurements into their management system – and they'll be surprised at the improvement in their project success rate.

Who's Responsible?

Even increased frequency of review doesn't solve the problem of our tendency to put lessons learned on hold. Capturing the lessons is only step one; when the process of documenting and organizing lessons learned is ignored or postponed, their value to the organization is lost. Part of the barrier is that the time and effort required to document and organize lessons learned feels like drudgery. Few people take pleasure in documenting events, including lessons learned.

The solution? Some organizations now take the responsibility of documenting lessons learned away from project managers and project teams. They make team members responsible for passing along project experiences and providing details about what they've learned, but they rely on a lessons-learned subject matter expert – a project knowledge management coordinator – to take care of and manage lessons learned. Lessons-learned management includes gathering, documenting, presenting for review and approval, updating, publishing, and making people within the organization aware of all lessons learned and how people can benefit from their use. This position should be part of a project management office or similar internal department. Organizations without a project management office or similar function focused on project procedures may want to keep the responsibility for lessons learned at the project level. Managing lessons learned is a full-time job. Let's look at what's required to effectively manage lessons learned.

Job Description

The project knowledge management coordinator, responsible for gathering and documenting lessons learned, should (Casey 2012):

- Take project-specific experiences obtained in project review sessions and word them in such a way that they become generic and can be applied throughout the entire organization.

- Review other sources for lessons learned, including meeting minutes and internal and external audit reports, to discover, capture, and document new lessons learned. Lessons learned need to be stored in a database and categorized so that they're easily searchable.

- Organize and present newly documented lessons learned to an internal review group for approval. The review group should be charged with the responsibility and authority to accept or reject new lessons learned as valuable to the organization.

- Update the lessons-learned database so that new lessons learned are published and made available to project teams throughout the organization.

- Keep the lessons-learned database up to date by removing lessons learned that have resulted in process improvements and are now part of documented procedures. Those lessons learned should have been saved in the back-up documentation/history/traceability matrix for the improved process. They can be especially important in preventing a repeat of history should a future manager want to try a previous failed approach when all who remember the history have moved out of the organization.

◆ Make people within the organization aware of what's included in the lessons-learned database and, more importantly, how project teams can use this information to their benefit.

DEDICATING A POSITION TO MANAGING LESSONS LEARNED provides value and support to the projects under way – freeing up and saving time.

REFERENCES

Ambler, Scott W. Agile Modeling Home Page. Accessed May 21, 2018, http://agilemodeling.com/.

Bonnie, Emily. 2015. "Complete Collection of Project Management Statistics 2015." Wrike.com blog. Accessed July 7, 2015, https://www.wrike.com/blog/complete-collection-project-management-statistics-2015/.

Bridges, Dianne N. 1999. "Project Portfolio Management: Ideas and Practices." In *Project Portfolio Management*, Lowell D. Dye and James S. Pennypacker, eds. Havertown, PA: Center for Business Practices.

Casey, John. 2012. Personal communication – details on the project knowledge management coordinator role.

Drucker, Peter. 1993. *The Practice of Management*. New York: HarperBusiness.

Gawande, Atul. 2010. *The Checklist Manifesto, First Edition*. New York: Picador Publishers.

Katzenbach, Jon, and Douglas K. Smith. 1994. *The Wisdom of Teams*. New York: HarperBusiness

PM Solutions Research. 2013. *The State of Project Portfolio Management*. Glen Mills, PA: PM Solutions.

PM Solutions Research. 2015. *The Project Manager Skills Benchmark*. Glen Mills, PA: PM Solutions.

PMI. 2013. *The Standard for Portfolio Management, Third Edition*. Newtown Square, PA: Project Management Institute.

PMI. 2015. "PMI Talent Triangle." Accessed May 17, 2018, https://www.pmi.org/-/media/pmi/documents/public/pdf/certifications/talent-triangle-flyer.pdf.

PMI. 2017. *A Guide to the Project Management Body of Knowledge (PMBOK® Guide), Sixth Edition.* Newtown Square, PA: Project Management Institute.

PMI. 2018. *PMI's Pulse of the Profession: Success in Disruptive Times.* Newtown Square, PA: Project Management Institute. Accessed May 2018 at https://www.pmi.org/-/media/pmi/documents/public/pdf/learning/thought-leadership/pulse/pulse-of-the-profession-2018.pdf.

Robbins, Stephen. 2005. *Organizational Behavior.* Upper Saddle River, NJ: Pearson Education.

Verma, Vijay. 1998. *Managing the Project Team: The Human Aspects of Project Management Volume 2.* Newtown Square, PA: Project Management Institute.

Verzuh, Eric. 2005. *Fast Forward MBA in Project Management, Second Edition.* New York: John Wiley & Sons.

SUGGESTED READINGS

Project Management Glossaries Online

Note that, as with any online resource, these URLs are likely to change without notice. A search in any Web search engine for "project management glossary" will yield these and many other similar sites.

- http://glossary.tenrox.com/
- http://maxwideman.com/pmglossary/
- https://en.wikipedia.org/wiki/Glossary_of_project_management

Introducing ... Project Management!

- Bonnie, Emily. 2015. "Complete Collection of Project Management Statistics 2015." Wrike.com blog. Accessed July 7, 2015, https://www.wrike.com/blog/complete-collection-project-management-statistics-2015/.
- Crawford, J. Kent, et al. 2008. *Project Management Roles and Responsibilities, Second Edition*. Glen Mills, PA: PM Solutions.
- Crawford, J. Kent, and Jeannette Cabanis-Brewin. 2005. *Optimizing Human Capital with a Strategic Project Office*. Boca Raton: Auerbach Books/CRC Press.
- Dinsmore, Paul, and Jeannette Cabanis-Brewin, eds. 2014. *AMA Handbook of Project Management, Fourth Edition*. New York: AMACOM.
- Pennypacker, James S., and Jeannette Cabanis-Brewin, eds. 2003. *What Makes a Good Project Manager*. Glen Mills, PA: PM Solutions.

◆ PM Solutions Research. 2015. *The Project Manager Skills Benchmark.* Glen Mills, PA: PM Solutions.

◆ Project Management Institute. 2017. *A Guide to the Project Management Body of Knowledge (PMBOK® Guide), Sixth Edition.* Newtown Square, PA: Project Management Institute.

◆ Project Management Institute. 2017. *PMI's Pulse of the Profession: Success in Disruptive Times.* Accessed May 21, 2018, https://www.pmi.org/-/media/pmi/documents/public/pdf/learning/thought-leadership/pulse/pulse-of-the-profession-2018.pdf. Newtown Square, PA: Project Management Institute.

◆ Whitten, Neal. 2007. *Neal Whitten's Let's Talk: More No-Nonsense Advice for Project Success.* Vienna, VA: Management Concepts.

Chapter 1: Selecting the Right Projects

◆ Cohen, Dennis J., and Robert J. Graham. 2000. *The Project Manager's MBA: How to Translate Project Decisions into Business Success.* San Francisco: Jossey-Bass.

◆ Crawford, J. Kent, with Jeannette Cabanis-Brewin. 2011. *The Strategic Project Office: A Guide to Improving Organizational Performance, Second Edition.* Boca Raton: Auerbach/CRC.

◆ Crawford, J. Kent, et al. 2008. *Seven Steps to Strategy Execution.* Glen Mills, PA: PM Solutions.

◆ PM Solutions Research. 2013. *The State of Project Portfolio Management.* Glen Mills, PA: PM Solutions.

◆ —. 2013. *Make the Commitment to Project Portfolio Management.* Glen Mills, PA: PM Solutions.

◆ Project Management Institute. 2013. *The Standard for Portfolio Management, Third Edition.* Newtown Square, PA: Project Management Institute.

◆ Project Management Institute. 2017. *A Guide to the Project Management Body of Knowledge (PMBOK® Guide), Sixth Edition.* Newtown Square, PA: Project Management Institute.

Chapter 2: Initiating the Project

◆ Dinsmore, Paul, and Terence J. Cooke-Davies. 2005. *The Right Projects Done Right: From Business Strategy to Successful Project Implementation.* Hoboken, NJ: John Wiley & Sons.

◆ Verzuh, Eric. 2005. *Fast Forward MBA in Project Management, Second Edition.* New York: John Wiley & Sons.

Chapter 3: Planning to Succeed

◆ Cleland, David I. 2004. *Field Guide to Project Management, Second Edition.* Hoboken, NJ: John Wiley & Sons.

◆ Lewis, James P. 2005. *Project Planning, Scheduling, and Control, Fourth Edition.* New York: McGraw-Hill.

Chapter 4: Project Cost and Budget

◆ Cohen, Dennis J., and Robert J. Graham. 2000. *The Project Manager's MBA: How to Translate Project Decisions into Business Success.* San Francisco: Jossey-Bass.

◆ Project Management Institute. 2017. *A Guide to the Project Management Body of Knowledge (PMBOK® Guide), Sixth Edition.* Newtown Square, PA: Project Management Institute.

◆ Rad, Parviz. 2001. *Project Estimating and Cost Management.* Vienna, VA: Management Concepts.

◆ Spiro, Herbert T. 1996. *Finance for the Non-Financial Manager, Fourth Edition.* Hoboken, NJ: John Wiley & Sons.

◆ Stewart, Rodney D. 1991. *Cost Estimating, Second Edition.* Hoboken, NJ: John Wiley & Sons.

Chapter 5: Scheduling the Project

◆ Fleming, Quentin, and Joel Koppelman. 2010. *Earned Value Project Management, Fourth Edition.* Newtown Square, PA: Project Management Institute.

◆ Kerzner, Harold. 2013. "Network Scheduling Techniques." In *Project Management: A Systems Approach to Planning, Scheduling and Controlling, Eleventh Edition.* Hoboken, NJ: John Wiley & Sons.

◆ Meredith, James, and Samuel Mantel. 2016. "Scheduling." In *Project Management, A Managerial Approach, Ninth Edition.* Hoboken, NJ: John Wiley & Sons.

◆ Project Management Institute. 2017. *A Guide to the Project Management Body of Knowledge (PMBOK® Guide), Sixth Edition.* Newtown Square, PA: Project Management Institute.

Chapter 6: The People Side of Project Management

◆ Crawford, J. Kent, and Jeannette Cabanis-Brewin. 2005. *Optimizing Human Capital with a Strategic Project Office.* Boca Raton: Auerbach Books/CRC Press.

◆ Demarco, Tom, and Timothy Lister. 2000. *Peopleware: Productive Projects and Teams, Second Edition.* New York: Dorset House.

◆ Lencioni, Patrick M. 2005. *Overcoming the Five Dysfunctions of a Team.* San Francisco: Jossey-Bass.

◆ Project Management Institute. 2017. *A Guide to the Project Management Body of Knowledge (PMBOK® Guide), Sixth Edition.* Newtown Square, PA: Project Management Institute.

◆ Verma, Vijay. 1996–98. *The Human Aspects of Project Management* series. Newtown Square, PA: Project Management Institute.

Chapter 7: Managing Project Risk

◆ Barkley, Bruce T. 2004. *Project Risk Management.* New York: McGraw-Hill.

◆ Hillson, David. 2014. "Project Risk Management in Practice." In *AMA Handbook of Project Management, Fourth Edition,* Paul Dinsmore and Jeannette Cabanis-Brewin, eds. New York: AMACOM.

◆ Pritchard, Carl L. 2015. *Risk Management: Concepts and Guidance.* Boca Raton, FL: CRC Press

◆ Project Management Institute. 2017. *A Guide to the Project Management Body of Knowledge (PMBOK® Guide), Sixth Edition.* Newtown Square, PA: Project Management Institute.

Chapter 8: Executing the Project

◆ Bossidy, Larry, Ram Charan, and Charles Burck. 2002. *Execution: The Discipline of Getting Things Done.* New York: Crown Business.

◆ Lewis, James P. 2005. *Project Planning, Scheduling, and Control, Fourth Edition.* New York: McGraw-Hill.

◆ Project Management Institute. 2017. *A Guide to the Project Management Body of Knowledge (PMBOK® Guide), Sixth Edition.* Newtown Square, PA: Project Management Institute.

Chapter 9: Monitoring and Controlling the Project

◆ Kerzner, Harold. 2013. *Project Management: A Systems Approach to Planning, Scheduling and Controlling, Eleventh Edition.* Hoboken, NJ: John Wiley & Sons.

◆ Meredith, James, and Samuel Mantel. 2016. "Scheduling." In *Project Management, A Managerial Approach, Ninth Edition.* Hoboken, NJ: John Wiley & Sons.

◆ Pinto, Jeffrey, and Jeffrey Trailer. 1999. *Essentials of Project Control*. Newtown Square, PA: Project Management Institute.

◆ Project Management Institute. 2017. *A Guide to the Project Management Body of Knowledge (PMBOK® Guide), Sixth Edition.* Newtown Square, PA: Project Management Institute.

◆ Streatfield, Philip. 2001. *The Paradox of Control in Organizations.* London: Routledge Publishing.

◆ Wren, Daniel. 2009. *The Evolution of Management Thought, Sixth Edition.* Hoboken, NJ: John Wiley & Sons.

Chapter 10: Closing the Project

◆ Gawande, Atul. 2010. *The Checklist Manifesto, First Edition.* New York: Picador Publishers.

Chapter 11: Lessons Learned . . . And Used

◆ Crawford, J. Kent, with Jeannette Cabanis-Brewin. 2011. *The Strategic Project Office: A Guide to Improving Organizational Performance, Second Edition.* Boca Raton: Auerbach/CRC.

◆ Crawford, J. Kent, et al. 2008. *Project Management Roles and Responsibilities, Second Edition.* Glen Mills, PA: PM Solutions.

INDEX

A

acceptance criteria, 18, 48
accept risk, 135, 137, 138
action parameters, 157
actual cost (AC), 171–72
actual cost of work performed
    (ACWP), 172
adaptive/agile approach, 46, 51
adaptive methods, 4
adjourning, 110
adjust schedule, 99–100
administrative guidelines, 42
agile methodology, 4
allies, 35
alternatives analysis, 70
ambiguity risk, 118
ambivalents, 36
analogous (analogy) estimate, 68
analysis, guided, 124–26
analyze schedule, 97–99
approvals, 45–46
approved project budget, 81
area of order (AOO), 59, 162
arrow diagramming method
    (ADM)/program evaluation
    and review technique (PERT),
    88–89
"art" of project management, 7–8

as-of-now status, 29
assumption log, 123
assumptions, 48, 77
audience for communication, 114
avoid risk, 134, 137

B

backward pass, 96–97
balance, 15, 19
baseline, 59–61
benefits closeout, 186
benefits of team membership, 106
bottom-up estimates, 67–68
budget, 60–61
budget at completion (BAC), 172
budgeted cost of work performed
    (BCWP), 172
budgeted cost of work scheduled
    (BCWS), 171
budget stage, 60
bundling, 176
business risk, 117
butterfly effect, 161–63

C

calendar time, 65
cause and effect diagrams, 124–26
cause-risk-effect format, 124

change control board, 150, 153

change management, 150, 153,
    154–55

change management board, 150,
    153

change pot, 155–56

change request form, 150, 152–55

change requests, 45–46

chaos, 59

charge codes, 185

checklist, closeout, 181–89

checklist on risk management,
    141–42

"classic" project management, 8–9

closing, 28–29, 179–80, 181

Closing Process Group, 2–3

closeout
    checklist, 181–89
    internal projects, 181
    phase, 180
    premature termination, 180–81
    project termination, 180–81

closure inspection, 164, 165–66

collaborating, 114

common ground, 108

communicating
    closeout, 188
    components of, 114–15
    during execution, 157–59
    lessons learned, 200

communication timing and
    frequency, 115

company confidential, 199–200

competencies, 10–11

compliance, 201

compromising, 114

computer-generated estimates, 71

configuration management board,
    150, 153

confirming estimate, 78

conflict resolution methods,
    113–14

connect emotionally, 108

consequences, unintended, 173

constraints, 48

Constructive Cost Model II
    (COCO-MO® II), 74

contingent response strategies, 137

contract closure, 182

contributions to corporation, 64

control, 174–76

Control Account Managers
    (CAMs), 63

Control Account Plan (CAP), 63

Control Accounts (CAs), 63

control action matrix, 174–75

control actions, 164

control costs, 80–81

controlling, 163–64

control schedule, 101

cost
    in baseline, 60
    of conformance, 70
    estimating, 66–68
    of nonconformance, 70
    over budget, 175–76
    overrun, 173
    of project management, 74
    of quality, 70
    in triple constraint, 49–51

cost baseline, project, 61–62
cost objects, 62–63
cost performance index (CPI), 172
costs, 62
cost variance (CV), 172–73
crash, 175
credibility, establishing, 108
critical path, 98
cultural factors, 6
customer closeout, 186–87
customer expectations, 148–49
customers, determining, 34

D
data
  collection, 166–70
  display, 167–70
  monitoring, 164
data analysis estimating, 69–71
decision guidelines, 42
decision trees, 132–33
defer expenditures, 79
define activities, 92
deliverables, 47, 52
deploy schedule, 100–01
de-scope, 78–79, 175
design reviews, 192
determine budget, 78–80
develop schedule, 95–101
direct costs, 63
discoveries, 192–94
discretionary dependencies, 93
documentation
  closing, 182
  review, 145–47

of risks, 123
scalability, 145
document control system, 39
driving predecessor, 96
driving successor, 97
driving task, 94
dropdown menu, 194
duration, 64–65
dynamic complexity, 133–34

E
early finish (EF), 95
early start (ES), 95
earned value (EV), 172
earned value management (EVM),
  170–73
efficiency, 11
effort, 64, 65
elapsed time, 65
eliminate the fat, 80
end inspection, 164, 165–66
engaging stakeholder, 30–39
enhance risk, 136
escalate risk, 134, 135–36
estimate, confirming, 78
estimate, validating, 77
estimate activity durations, 94–95
estimate costs, 76–78
estimates, 67–68
estimating process, 60–61
estimating tools, 68–69
event and risk, 117, 120
evidence, 108
evolution of project management,
  8–9

exclusions, 48

executing process, 28–29

Executing Process Group, 2–3

expectations, customer, 36, 148–49

expected monetary value, 132–33

expenditures, 79

expensed budget items, 60

exploit risk, 136, 137

external stakeholders, 35

F

fast track, 175

fear, 72–73, 173–74

features, delete, 176

financial closing, 185

finish-to-finish (FF), 94

finish-to-start (FS), 93

fishbone diagram, 124–26

fit, 15, 18

Five Whys, 124

fixed costs, 64

forcing, 114

formality in project management, 189–90

forming, 109

forward pass, 95–96

free float, 98–99

functional approach, 53

funding, additional, 176

G

Gantt charts, 86–88

goals of stakeholders, 36

Godzilla bone diagram, 124–26

ground rules, 42

groups, 105–06

guided analysis, 124–26

Guide to the Project Management Body of Knowledge, A (PMBOK® Guide)

on baseline, 59

on cost management, 74–75

standards, 1–4

on WBS, 51

GWOP, 71

H

history of project management, 4–5

human dimension, 115

human factors, 6

I

identify early, 162

Identify Risks, 120, 123–26

impact of risk, 73–74, 120

Implement Risk Responses, 121, 189–39

indirect costs, 63–64

individual project risk, 117

individual versus team, 104–05

influence/impact balancing matrix, 32, 33

influencing, 10, 107–08

information, adequate, 73

initial budget stage, 60

initiating process, 28–29

Initiating Process Group, 1–3

in situ review, 164–65

intellectual database, 38–39, 40, 41
intent in communication, 115
internal stakeholders, 34
Ishikawa diagram, 124–26
issue log, 123
issue versus risk, 118
iterative approximation, 66
iterative methods, 4
IT projects, 5

J
just-in-time strategy, 147

K
kickoff meetings, 39–41, 43
Knowledge Areas, 2, 4
knowledge management
    coordinator, 202–03

L
labor, lower-cost, 176
lag time, 99–100
late finish (LF), 97
leader consistency, 157
leadership, 6, 7, 10, 109
lead time, 100
legal review, 186
lessons learned
    acting on, 189
    cataloguing, 190
    communicating, 200
    methodology, 192–99
    monthly meeting, 200–01
logistics closeout, 186

M
mandatory dependencies, 93
media, choosing, 115
meeting guidelines, 42
message contents, 115
milestone chart, 90
milestones, 156
minutes, meeting, 156–57
mitigate/enhance risk, 138
mitigate risk, 135
monitoring, 162–67
monitoring and controlling
    process, 28–29
Monitoring and Controlling
    Process Group, 2–3
Monitor Risks, 121, 139–42
mutual accountability, 106

N
negative lag, 100
negative risks, 134–35
net present value management, 176
network diagrams, 88
network schedules, 88–89
neutral engagement, 37
"new project management," 9
nine-block matrix, 127–28
nominal group technique, 123
non-event risks, 117
norming, 110

O
objectors, 107–08
opponents, 35–36

order of magnitude approach, 67

organizational kickoff meeting, 40–41

outcomes, 6

outsource, 176

overall project risk, 117, 137–38

overhead costs, 64

P

pairwise comparison matrix, 128–30

parametric estimate, 68

patterns, breaking, 36

peer review, 145

people issues, 193

perceptions, 194–99

performance reports, 185

performance-to-date, 172–73

performing, 110

Perform Qualitative Risk Analysis, 121

Perform Quantitative Risk Analysis, 121

Perform Risk Analysis, 126–34

personal attributes, 11

personal self-assessment, 10

phase closeout, 180

phased approach, 53

phase review, 164, 165, 166

phases, 2, 29

PIDOOMA, 71

plan, having a, 162

plan cost management, 75–76

plan, do, check, and act (PDCA) cycle, 164, 165

planned value (PV), 171

planners, inexperienced, 72

planning phase, 143–44

planning process, 28–29

Planning Process Group, 1–3

Plan Risk Management, 120, 121–23

Plan Risk Responses, 121, 134–38

plan schedule management, 91–92

portfolio management, 9, 14–17

portfolio manager, 20–22

positive risks, 135–37

precedence diagramming method/ critical path method (PDM/ CPM), 89, 95–98

predecessor, 92–94, 96, 100

predecessor tasks, 97

predictive approach, 46

predictive-type project, 51

premature termination closeout, 180–81

present-value approach, 79

price, 65–66

primary activity, 93

priority matrix, 50–51

probability, 120

problems, reporting, 149–50

problem solving, 114, 156

problem-solving skills, 10

Process Groups, 1–3

process reviews, 192

product approach, 53

productivity, 80

product scope versus project scope, 46–47

Program Evaluation and Review
 Technique (PERT), 68–69
profit, 66
program management, 9
project audit, 145
project baseline budget, 60
project change log, 153–55
project charter, 25–27, 40–41
project cost baseline, 61–62
project dashboard, 168
project deliverable, 52
project file, 38–39, 40, 41
project justification template, 18
project management
 "art," 7–8
 "classic," 8–9
 cost of, 74
 evolution of, 8–9
 knowledge, 11
 "new," 9
 plan, 49
 processes, 28–29
 "science," 7–8
 "traditional," 8–9
project management information
 system (PMIS), 49, 71
Project Management Institute, 1
project management office, 9
project manager role, 9–10
project office, 189
project portfolio management
 (PPM), 13–14, 21–23
project repository, 38–39, 40, 41
project risk management, 119,
 120–21, 122

projects, troubled, 144
project schedule, 57
project scope statement, 51
project scope versus product scope,
 46–47
project selection, 17–19
project status report, 157
project status reviews, 192
project summary view, 90
project termination closeout,
 180–81
project workbook, 38–39, 40, 41
proposed budget stage, 60
pull concept, 107
pure risk, 117
PURGE, 71

Q
qualitative risk analysis, 126–30
quantitative risk analysis, 130–34
questionnaires, 194–99

R
reflective activities, 77
relationship arrows, 93–94
renegotiate, 176
replan, 175
reporting template, 140–41
reports, performance, 185
reserve analysis, 70
resistant engagement, 37
resource assignment matrix
 (RAM), 56–57
resource bar chart, 169
resources, additional, 176

resources, non-committed, 72
responsibilities of communicating, 115
responsibility, 41
review, legal, 186
reviews, 192
risk
  accept, 135, 137, 138
  on agenda, 156
  assigning, 140
  avoid, 134, 137
  components of, 120
  discussing, 140
  enhance, 136
  escalate, 134–36
  exploit, 136, 137
  mitigate, 135
  mitigate/enhance, 138
  owning, 118
  planning for, 73–74
  share, 136
  transfer, 135
  transfer/share, 137–38
risk, ambiguity, 118
risk, business, 117
risk, event-based, 117
risk, high-level, 48
risk, individual project, 117
risk, negative, 134–35
risk, non-event, 117
risk, overall project, 117
risk, positive, 135–37
risk, pure, 117
risk, speculative, 117
risk, variability, 117–18

risk appetite, 122
risk documentation, 123
risk event impact, 73–74
risk event value, 127–28
risk exposure, 127–28
risk log, 123, 151
risk management, 118–20, 140
risk management checklist, 141–42
risk register, 123
risk severity, 127–28
risk threshold, 122
risk versus issue, 118
role, 41
role of portfolio manager, 20–22
role of project manager, 9–10
rolling wave, 58, 62
root cause analysis, 124
rough-order-of-magnitude (ROM) assessment, 67, 76, 130
run chart, 169

S
sales, general, and administrative (SG&A) costs, 64
scalability, 145
schedule, 49–51, 83–89, 175
schedule management processes, 90–101
schedules, network, 88–89
schedule variance (SV), 173
scheduling problems, 85–86
"science" of project management, 7–8

scope, 46–47, 49–51, 176
scope change request/impact form, 152
scope management plan, 45–46
scope statement, 45–48
security, closing, 182, 185
self-assessment, personal, 10
sensitivity analysis, 131–32
sequence activities, 92–94
shared purpose, 106
share risk, 136
simulations, 133–34
smoothing, 114
software estimating, 71
speculative risk, 117
sponsors, 33–34
stages, 2, 29
stakeholder engagement, 30–39
stakeholder management plan, 37–38
stakeholder register, 32
stakeholders
  external, 35
  identifying, 31–36
  internal, 34
  key, 33–34, 37, 40–41
standard, 167–68
start-to-finish (SF), 94
start-to-start (SS), 93
status meetings, 156–59
status report, 158
storming, 109, 110–13
Strategic and Business Management, 7
subject matter experts (SMEs), 68

subject matter groups (SMGs), 68
subordinate activity, 93
subordinate tasks, 94
sub-processes, 2
successor, 92–94, 100
successor tasks, 95
supportive engagement, 37
SWAG, 71
SWOT (strengths, weaknesses, opportunities, and threats), 123

T
Talent Triangle, 8
team
  charter, 41–42
  closeout, 188–89
  definition, 104
  development stages, 108–10
  kickoff meeting, 41
  membership, 106
  organizational chart, 41
  when to use, 105
team/stakeholder roster, 41
teams versus groups, 105–06
Technical Project Management, 7
technological savvy, 11
template for project justification, 18
termination, early, 188
terminology, standardized, 194
terms, defining, 126–27
threats, 134–35
three-point estimates, 68–69
time off, eliminate, 176

timing and frequency of communication, 115
tolerances, monitoring, 157
tools for project portfolio management, 22–23
top-down estimates, 67
tornado diagram, 131–32
total float (TF), 98
total slack, 98
"traditional" project management, 8–9
transfer risk, 135
transfer/share risk, 137–38
transition, 187
trigger conditions, 123
trim expenditures, 79
triple constraint, 49–51

U
uncertainty, 73–74
unknown-unknowns, 118

utility, 15, 18–19

V
validate estimate, 77
validate schedule, 99
value engineering, 78
variability risk, 117–18
variable costs, 64
variance, 162–63
vendor/contractor, 185

W
waste, 6
"what if," 70
WIIFM, 36, 148
withdrawing (non-confrontational), 113
work breakdown structure (WBS), 45–46, 51–56
work package, 52
work performance, 29–30

ABOUT THE AUTHORS & EDITOR

WILLIAM P. ATHAYDE, J.D., PMP, Senior Instructor, PM College. As a senior faculty member of the PM College, Bill's responsibilities include classroom and virtual training, course development, and consulting on training issues as well as project management. Bill gained his project management experience working in oil spill and hazardous materials remediation projects, construction, systems development and integration, and as the program manager of a team composed of 120 representatives of fourteen federal agencies, six state governments, and industry. He also served as COO of a 165-person environmental services company in Virginia. Bill has authored various papers and spoken on disaster recovery planning and operations, project and program team dynamics, CAMEO (Computer-Aided Management of Emergency Operations), and emergency response. He is a member of the State Bar of Texas.

DEBORAH BIGELOW CRAWFORD, PMP, President, PM College. Debbie is responsible for the fiscal management and quality assurance of the PM College program. Her previous experience as Executive Director of the Project Management Institute (PMI) has given her the expertise to manage and develop new initiatives and programs for this fast-paced and innovative project management training company. Debbie also serves as Executive Vice President of Project Management Solutions, Inc. (PM Solutions). She has served as a contributing editor to *PM Network, Chief Project Officer,* and *Optimize* magazines and has published numerous papers in PMI's Congress Proceedings and presented internationally on a wide range of project management issues.

RUTH ELSWICK, PMP, Senior Instructor, PM College. In addition to teaching the PM College curriculum, Ruth contributes her extensive project management experience in curriculum development and instructor mentoring. Ruth gained her project management experience working in FDA-regulated industries. She has held various project management positions for major pharmaceutical, biotech, and medical device organizations. These positions included managing a multi-million-dollar global biotech start-up as well as establishing a project office and the implementation of a project selection process. Ruth also currently serves as an adjunct professor in project management at Florida International University.

PAUL LOMBARD, PMP, a Library of Congress registered expert in Project Management, has over 25 years' experience in the project management space and is the owner of Global Training Group, LLC, a strategic program and project training and consulting company in Virginia Beach Virginia. Paul's responsibilities include classroom facilitation, course development, and project and quality management consulting and instructor mentorship. Paul gained his project management experience as a project and program manager for the U.S. government. He has also worked with many for profit and non-governmental not-for-profit organizations around the world since leaving government. He is a certified master trainer and curriculum developer and has developed numerous on-site and distance-learning training courses in project management, leadership, team skills, core facilitation, quality management, program management, complex project management, and strategic management. Paul was awarded a Distinguished Civil Service Medal for his project work while assigned as an internal consultant to the Department of the Navy.

CPSIA information can be obtained
at www.ICGtesting.com
Printed in the USA
JSHW041257051021
19318JS00001B/2